MORE STRANGE BUT TRUE FOOTBALL STORIES

An injured player helps his team win while lying on a blanket; a quarterback catches his own pass; a championship game is played in a blizzard. These and 25 other stories show that in the world of football fact can be stranger than fiction.

MORE
STRANGE BUT TRUE
FOOTBALL STORIES

compiled and edited by
Zander Hollander

illustrated with photographs

Random House • New York

PHOTOGRAPH CREDITS: John Biever, 58, 148–149; Vernon Biever, 7, 20, 98, 101; Bowling Green State University (by Cliff Boutelle), 129; University of Michigan, 113, 117; University of New Mexico, 94–95; University of Oklahoma, 62; Ken Regan—Camera 5, 2–3, 24, 139; University of the South, 142; Texas Christian University, 81; United Press International, endpapers, 13, 14, 17, 26, 33, 44, 48, 50, 61, 65, 66, 74, 102, 109, 124, 126; Wide World Photos, 36, 56–57, 59, 78–79, 86.
Cover art by Gil Cohen.

Library of Congress Cataloging in Publication Data
Hollander, Zander, comp.
More strange but true football stories.
(Punt, pass & kick library, 19)
SUMMARY: Recounts twenty-eight humorous, frustrating, disappointing, and exciting moments in football history from 1892 to the present.
1. Football—History—Juvenile literature.
[1. Football—History] I. Title.
GV950.7.H64 1973   796.33′2′09   73-4990
ISBN 0-394-82607-8
ISBN 0-394-92607-2 (lib. bdg.)

Contents

Introduction

The letter came from a young reader in a small town in the state of Washington. "I enjoyed your book *Strange But True Football Stories*," he wrote, "and I want to know whether you have any more of them."

Indeed there are more of them. Thanks to an occasional fan who forwards an oddity, an alert sports writer who seizes on the bizarre, and dozens of other sources, we have come up with another set of tales that illustrate the unpredictable bounce of the football. Our job was to track them down, separate fact from fiction and retell the ones that make the most entertaining reading.

The stories will take you through snow and hurricane; on a historic airplane trip; through a comedy of errors; to the first night game, and to other happenings. You will meet Joe Namath, Paul Hornung, Bill Kilmer, Johnny Unitas, Fran Tarkenton—and dozens of players you never heard of before.

The editor wishes to acknowledge the contribution of David Schulz, who did much of the research and writing, and thanks to Paul Levine for being the back-up man.

Zander Hollander
Baldwin, New York

MORE
STRANGE BUT TRUE
FOOTBALL STORIES

1.
Photo Finish

The game was between the Oakland Raiders and the New York Jets. It was November 17, 1968, and the home-team Raiders were defending champions of the American Football League. They needed to beat the Jets to stay in contention in the AFL's Western Division. If the Jets won, they would be sure of a tie for their first Eastern Division championship. Football fans around the nation—and especially in New York —tuned in the big game. It began at 4:30 New York time. Many families made plans to have a Sunday supper around the television since the game would not be over until nearly 7 o'clock.

Right from the start, the game was close. The quarterbacks, the Jets' Joe Namath and the Raiders' Daryle Lamonica, were two of the best in football. In the

10

first half, Lamonica threw two touchdown passes and Namath led the Jets to two field goals and a touchdown. As the teams left the field at half time, the scoreboard read: Raiders 14, Jets 12.

The first half had been rough and filled with penalties. Most television fans didn't notice, but the game was also taking a little longer than usual. Penalties, measurements for first downs and injury time-outs were adding a few minutes here and there to the usual playing time. After the half-time festivities, the teams returned. Midway through the third quarter the Jets scored a touchdown. Then the Raiders drove 80 yards for a touchdown of their own. They ran the ball across the goal on the extra-point attempt, earning two points under the AFL's rules and stretching their lead to three points. The score was 22–19.

Early in the fourth quarter the television fans in New York got a chance to cheer. The Raiders had driven deep into New York territory when rookie Charlie Smith fumbled only one yard from the goal line. New York's Gerry Philbin recovered the ball at the 3, ending the Raiders' scoring threat. Then Namath fired a pass to Don Maynard at midfield. On the next play Namath hit Maynard again for 50 yards and a touchdown. The Jets went ahead 26–22. A few minutes later the Jets' Jim Turner booted his third field goal, putting New York ahead, 29–22. Now there was joy in televisionland.

There were still almost nine minutes left, and the

Raiders were fired up. They had to win this game. Quarterback Lamonica needed another score, and he soon got it on a 22-yard scoring pass to Fred Biletnikoff. This time the Raiders kicked the extra point and it was good, tying the game at 29–all.

Now the Jets had the ball with almost four minutes left to play. Joe Namath began to drive his team upfield on running plays and short passes. He was using up the clock so that if New York scored, Oakland would have too little time to come back. The Jets were stopped short of a touchdown, but with one minute and five seconds remaining, Turner kicked his fourth field goal to put the Jets ahead, 32–29.

The TV viewers had learned that a game like this is never over until the gun sounds, so they stayed close to their sets. They watched Oakland's Charlie Smith return the Jets' kickoff to his 22-yard-line. Next Lamonica completed a 20-yard pass to Smith. On the following play the referee walked off a 15-yard penalty against the Jets. The Raiders had already marched to the New York 43, and there was still plenty of time left.

Jet fans were sitting on the edge of their seats, waiting for the next play. But the next thing they saw on their screens was a station break. Then a commercial. They hoped that the game would return before anything exciting happened. But then the familiar peacock appeared on the screen and viewers were informed that the following program would appear in

Heidi looks worried as football fans impatiently wait for the end of the Jets-Raiders game.

living color. The following program? Where was the football game?

There followed the opening scenes of a children's television special—the story of Heidi. Football fans in New York and across the country were furious. How could they find out how the game ended? The NBC switchboard in New York lighted up with so many calls that it literally exploded. Even the emergency police number in New York was tied up with complaining football fans. The network decided to return

Charlie Smith (23) is mobbed after scoring the winning touchdown for the Raiders—off the screen.

the game to the air, but the decision was made too late. By then, the game was over and the children watching "Heidi" were irritated by the interruption.

Unknown to the fans, a tense drama had been going on in the NBC studios. The television executives knew that there were millions of children expecting to see "Heidi" at 7 o'clock. And if the program didn't start on time, something would have to be left out. When the Jets scored and went ahead with only a minute left, the man in charge decided that Oakland wouldn't have time to score. He ordered "Heidi" to begin at 7 o'clock as scheduled.

What did happen? The last play on TV had shown the Raiders on the New York 43. But as soon as "Heidi" went on the air, Lamonica threw to Smith again, this time for a touchdown. The extra point attempt was good, the Raiders were ahead, 36–32. The game still wasn't over, though. On the kickoff, Oakland's Preston Ridlehuber recovered a Jet fumble and scurried two yards for another Oakland touchdown.

For the television fans the game had "ended" with the Jets winning, 32–29. Imagine their surprise when they learned that Oakland had scored 14 points in the last minute to win by a score of 43–32.

From that day on, Heidi was a nasty word to football fans. They couldn't complain about the little Swiss girl of the story, but they never forgot the day Heidi came on a minute too early.

2.
One-Time Quarterback

Head coach Otto Graham read off the starting line-up for the College All-Stars. At quarterback he called the name of Ron VanderKelen. In a few minutes, VanderKelen would be running out onto the turf at Soldiers Field in Chicago to lead a bunch of college kids against the Green Bay Packers. This game between the best collegians and the champions of the National Football League was played every August. The year before, in 1962, the Packers had whipped the All-Stars, 42–20. Now, in 1963, Green Bay was planning to give the college boys another lesson.

VanderKelen knew all about the Packers. He had grown up in Preble, Wisconsin, just outside Green Bay. And like many kids there, he had always wanted to play for the Packers. He was a good enough high school player to get a scholarship to the University of Wisconsin. But in his first two varsity seasons, he mostly sat on the bench, playing only 37 minutes in 20 games.

In his senior year, though, VanderKelen got his chance at quarterback. In a spectacular season he led the Badgers to the Rose Bowl. Wisconsin lost the game to Southern California, but VanderKelen had one of the greatest days in Rose Bowl history. He com-

Ron VanderKelen looks for a receiver during the 1963 Rose Bowl.

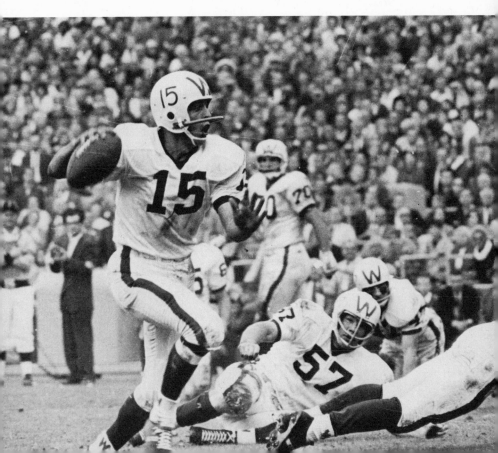

pleted 33 of 48 passes for 401 yards and two touchdowns. He scored a third touchdown himself.

Despite his outstanding performance at Wisconsin, the Packers didn't select VanderKelen in the annual player draft. In fact, no professional team drafted him. The pro scouts credited much of VanderKelen's belated success to his outstanding pass-catching end, Pat Richter, who later became a professional star. The scouts simply didn't think that VanderKelen, who had done nothing much until his senior year, was worth the gamble.

So August 2, 1963, would be Vandy's one chance to show what he could do against a pro team. At least he could let the Packers know what they were missing.

Early in the first quarter the All-Star offense got the ball for the first time, on its own 8-yard line. On third down, the All-Star ball-carrier fumbled and the Packers recovered. Three plays later Packer fullback Jimmy Taylor burst into the end zone for the touchdown. The Packers were ahead 7–0.

Later in the quarter VanderKelen rallied the All-Stars. Using short passes and running plays against the great Packer defense, he moved the ball into Packer territory. The drive fizzled on the Green Bay 14-yard line, but Bob Jencks kicked a field goal to make the score a respectable 7–3.

In the second quarter the All-Stars got the ball on the Packer 29-yard line when Tom Janik intercepted a pass. On second down, VanderKelen picked his Wisconsin teammate Pat Richter out of the crowd, completing a pass to the 6-yard line. On the next play Larry Ferguson carried over from there to give the All-Stars the lead at 10–7.

The Packers tied the score with a 21-yard field goal before the half ended. Thanks to VanderKelen among others, the All-Stars had held the Packers even so far.

In the tradition of All-Star games, a different All-Star quarterback started the second half. The collegians got one drive started early, but the Packers' Herb Adderley stopped the threat singlehanded by intercepting a pass and returning it to the All-Star 20-yard line. The All-Star defense rose to the occasion, holding the Packers and forcing them to try a field goal. The attempt was wide and the score remained 10–10.

Later in the quarter, Green Bay was on the move again, straight toward the All-Star goal line. But the usually sure-handed Taylor fumbled on the 12-yard line, and Danny Brabham recovered for the All-Stars. The plucky college team continued to surprise the NFL champs. They kept the ball on the ground and marched 62 yards before bogging down. Early in the fourth quarter Jencks came on to try another field goal. It was good, and the All-Stars had the lead once again, 13–10.

But the champion Packers came roaring back. Elijah Pitts ripped off a 43-yard run to bring the ball deep into All-Star territory. With the ball on the 17-yard line it seemed that the Pack would soon be ahead again. Then Pitts was dropped for an 8-yard loss, and a screen pass lost another six yards. Green Bay tried

VanderKelen is interviewed after the All-Star game as coach Otto Graham (left) looks on.

another field goal, and again it was wide.

With only 4:15 left to play, the Packers were losing, 13–10. But Green Bay was dangerous to the last minute. The contest had not yet been decided.

On the sidelines, coach Graham called Vander-Kelen and told him to go back into the game. Graham instructed Vandy to call only running plays. Use up as much time as possible, he said, and pass only if absolutely necessary.

Starting from their own 20-yard line after the missed field goal, the All-Stars gained six yards on the first two running plays. On third down and four yards to go, VanderKelen decided the pass was necessary. He called a play to his favorite receiver—Pat Richter. Pat worked his way free along the sideline, and VanderKelen hit him with a bullet-like pass. Richter put a fake on Packer defender Jesse Whittenton, escaped his flailing tackle attempt and sprinted down the sidelines 74 yards for a touchdown. Jencks' extra point made it All-Stars 20, Packers 10. VanderKelen's last touchdown pass proved to be the deciding play. Green Bay managed to score another touchdown before the clock ran out, and the final score was 20–17.

But by then the All-Star victory was secure, engineered by Ron VanderKelen, the quarterback nobody wanted. After his All-Star performance, the Minnesota Vikings signed Ron. He was a Viking for five years and later played with the Atlanta Falcons and Edmonton in the Canadian Football League before settling into a career in the advertising business in Minneapolis.

When he retired VanderKelen did so with the knowledge that he had fooled a lot of people, especially the pro scouts. They're supposed to know better.

3.
Aerial Show

When the New Orleans Saints and the St. Louis Cardinals met on November 2, 1969, neither team was going anywhere. Worse yet, their quarterbacks were both being booed by hometown fans and their jobs were in jeopardy. No one could have predicted that these two struggling players would set any records that day.

Billy Kilmer, the Saints' signal-caller, had been a standout athlete at little Citrus High School in Azusa, California. From there he had gone on to UCLA, where his achievements as a running back made him the number one draft choice of the San Francisco 49ers.

But when he reached the pros, his career seemed to be all downhill. As a rookie running back in 1961, Bill scored ten touchdowns. The next year he scored only six. Then his world nearly collapsed. Injured in a near-fatal auto accident, he sat out the entire 1963 campaign. When he returned to active duty in 1964, he carried the ball only 36 times and failed to score. The next year Bill didn't even play in the NFL. His career seemed to be over. In 1966 he became a third-string quarterback. This seemed like a second chance, but he carried the ball only three times all season and threw just 16 passes. It seemed unlikely that Bill would last much longer in the NFL. But then he was picked up by the New Orleans Saints. On this brand-new team staffed with castoffs from other clubs, Bill emerged as the starting quarterback. Now he was playing, but the Saints were among the worst teams in the NFL. They won only three games their first year and four the second year. The New Orleans fans were impatient—they wanted a winner, and most of all they wanted a winning quarterback.

Quarterback Charley Johnson of the Cardinals was a Texan. At New Mexico State he had quarterbacked his team to an unbeaten season in 1960. In his early years with St. Louis, he was considered one of the better quarterbacks in the NFL. He was as brilliant off the field as he was on it, and was studying for a master's degree in chemical engineering in the offseason. In 1966 he was leading the Cardinals toward a division title (with a 7–1 record) when he was injured. The team fell apart and lost the title. Johnson spent the

next two years in military service. When he returned in 1969, things were not the same. The Cardinals were losing, and like Kilmer, Charley was being booed by his fans.

So, when the two teams met, both Kilmer and Johnson were trying to hold on to their jobs. New Orleans struck first as Kilmer threw a 25-yard touchdown pass to Dave Parks. Johnson replied with a 32-yard aerial to Dave Williams to tie the score. In the second period, Johnson found Williams in the end zone again to send St. Louis into the lead. Kilmer came back with touchdown passes to Ernie Wheelwright and Dan Abramowicz. The Saints also got a field goal and finished the half with a 23–14 lead.

In the second half Kilmer heaved his fourth touchdown pass, to Don Shy. Then the Saints scored on a plunge by Wheelwright, and Kilmer threw his fifth TD of the game, to Abramowicz. Now it was 44–14, New Orleans. But Johnson refused to give up. He threw his third TD pass, to John Gilliam. Then Kilmer fired his sixth!

The score was 51–21, with 13 minutes left to play. The home crowd of 46,718 in St. Louis was disgusted, and many started to head for the exits. But Charley Johnson still had something left in his right arm. He proceeded to rifle three more touchdown passes, two to

Cardinal quarterback Charley Johnson goes back to pass.

Williams and one to Roy Shivers, before time ran out.

The Saints had won, 51–42. Quarterbacks Kilmer and Johnson had each thrown six touchdown passes! Their total of twelve set a National Football League record for most touchdown passes in a game.

Stranger than the record itself, however, were the quarterbacks who set them. The fans stopped booing for a day, but records or not, Kilmer and Johnson were just about washed up with their teams. On opening day of the 1970 season Johnson was playing for the Houston Oilers. And a year later Kilmer was wearing the uniform of the Washington Redskins. Johnson was soon replaced as starting quarterback for the Oilers. But Kilmer, whose career had seemed to be all downhill, became the starting quarterback for the Redskins and helped lead them all the way to the Super Bowl in 1972.

The Saints' Billy Kilmer gets set to throw over the hands of a Cardinal defender.

4.
Night Game

Football began as a game to be played by school boys on cool autumn afternoons. When colleges started challenging other colleges, the games began to draw a few spectators. It was easy for students to take an afternoon off to see a football game, but it was much more difficult for working men and women. Before the turn of the century, the work week was from seven in the morning to seven at night, six days a week. That didn't leave many daylight hours for playing or watching a favorite sport. In some parts of the country, playing games on Sunday was frowned on, too.

In the 1880s and '90s people began to use electric lighting in their homes. It wasn't long before a football fan somewhere began to dream about playing the game after dark—under electric lights. At first it was only a dream—imagine the number of bulbs that would be needed to light a football field and the amount of electricity that would be used. But soon enough, somebody was bound to try it.

The first documented night game was played in Des Moines, Iowa, on October 5, 1900. Iowa was not major football territory in those days (the leading college teams were Harvard, Yale and Princeton—all in the East). But the supporters of Drake University in Des Moines arranged for three rows of electric arc lights to be placed on each side of the university field. Each row had 50 bulbs. Then they invited Grinnell College of Grinnell, Iowa, to travel to Des Moines to play the Drake team.

On the night of the game a crowd of 2,000 turned out, attracted as much by the novel experiment as by the football. The lighting hardly compared with that in a modern stadium, but the yard markers stood out clearly. The dimness of the lighting even played a part in Grinnell's strategy for the game. They had the smaller, lighter team, so they planned to do a lot of faking in the backfield, hoping that it would be hard for the Drake players to see who finally got the ball.

The strategy wasn't successful. Grinnell was held scoreless in the first half, while the bigger Drake team picked up a touchdown (worth five points) and an extra point, to lead 6–0. The forward pass had not yet been invented, and in a game of straight blocking and tackling, Drake's greater strength made the difference.

At the half, the teams retreated to opposite corners of the field (locker rooms were a later development). A newspaper report revealed something about the quality of the lighting. The coaches met at midfield to talk about the first half, according to the story. Then they joined their teams in the end zones, "hunting for their men to congratulate them on their good behaviour."

Neither team scored in the second half, so Drake had a 6–0 victory.

The experiment was so successful that Drake scheduled another night game for the following week. The student newspaper announced the second night game like this: "Good officials have been secured, the lighting facilities will be improved and more bleachers are to be erected. Football by electric light seems to be a 'go' at least as long as the weather's warm."

5.
Big Kick

Tom Dempsey didn't look much like a football player. He stood 6-foot-1 and weighed 265 pounds. The weight hung on him in layers, and he looked like a piece of overstuffed furniture. His teammates called him "Sofa." Dempsey also had no right hand and only half a right foot—the result of birth defects.

But Dempsey did play football, as a defensive end in high school and junior college, and as a place-kicker in the National Football League. Halfway through the 1970 season, Dempsey was having his problems while playing with the New Orleans Saints. He had made only five of fifteen field goal tries in his first seven games. New Orleans was also having its difficulties, winning only one game in seven, the team's worst start ever.

On November 8, the Detroit Lions came to New Orleans expecting an easy game against the Saints. The Lions had a 5–2 record and were in the running for the postseason playoffs.

The 66,910 loyal Saints fans filed into Sugar Bowl Stadium wondering how big the final score was going to be for the other team. But during the first quarter they were pleasantly surprised when Dempsey trotted out onto the field, wearing his specially built shoe, and kicked a 29-yard field goal to give the Saints a 3–0 lead.

Detroit bounced back in the next period, marching 80 yards for a score. The touchdown came on a 10-yard run by Mel Farr, and the Lions were ahead, 7–3.

Late in the second quarter Dempsey was sitting on the bench adjusting the special shoe on his right foot. The shoe, made by an orthopedic company in California, had a 1¾-inch-thick leather plate on the front end to provide a surface for striking the football.

Suddenly there was a roar from the crowd. Detroit's Nick Eddy had fumbled a punt and the Saints' Elijah Pitts had recovered on the Lion 39-yard line. There were 45 seconds left in the half. Half a minute later Dempsey was walking onto the field. His shoe was properly laced once again, and he proceeded to kick a 27-yard field goal to make the score 7–6. The Saints trailed by only a point.

The third quarter provided more scoring, but most of it was for the wrong team. Lion quarterback Bill

Tom Dempsey kicks a first-half field goal against the Lions.

Munson threw a two-yard scoring pass to Charlie Sanders, and Detroit went ahead 14–6. Dempsey had one field goal try blocked, but he made good on an eight-yard attempt to make the score 14–9.

It looked like another hard-fought loss for the New Orleans team. Then New Orleans linebacker Jackie Burkett intercepted a Lion pass, giving the Saints the ball on the Lion 34-yard line. With just under seven minutes to go, Tom Barrington scored from the 3-yard line. To the surprise of the fans, the Saints were ahead 16–14. Could they beat the Lions?

Detroit wasn't about to give up. The Lions sent in young back-up quarterback Greg Landry to replace Bill Munson. Starting from his 14-yard line, Landry began to move the team down the field. He threw passes to Larry Walton, Earl McCulloch and tight end Sanders. He gave the ball to Mel Farr and carried it himself.

As the Lions passed midfield it was time for Detroit's place-kicker, Errol Mann, to get nervous. Time was running out, and Mann knew he might be called upon for a field goal try. The 6-foot, 200-pound Mann watched with a blank stare from the sidelines. "I was getting my thoughts together," he would say later. "I was just hoping they'd get the ball over the 40. I was nervous, but there was no doubt in my mind I'd make it."

The Lions kept driving, down to the New Orleans 16. With 38 seconds left, Landry kept the ball and

34

drove over right guard for seven yards, down to the Saints' 9. It was third down. Mel Farr carried the ball to the left on the next play in order to place the ball directly in front of the goal posts.

Detroit took its last time-out with 14 seconds left. Mann rushed onto the field. His kick was straight and true. The score was Detroit 17, New Orleans 16. And there were only eleven seconds left to play.

The crowd had seen a good football game, but it seemed the Saints had lost again. Fans began getting their belongings together as Detroit kicked off to the Saints. Al Dodd returned the ball to the New Orleans 28, running out of bounds with eight seconds left.

The Saints' offensive unit jogged back onto the field. Quarterback Bill Kilmer called the play. A pass to Dodd was good for 17 yards, and he was pushed out of bounds on his own 45-yard line. The clock showed two seconds left.

New Orleans coach J. D. Roberts—who had been named head coach less than a week before the game—looked at the clock, then at the scoreboard. He realized there was only one thing to do. He sent in the field goal unit with Jackie Burkett to center, Joe Scarpati to hold and Tom Dempsey to kick.

Scarpati placed the ball down on the 37-yard line —his own 37! The goal posts were 63 yards away. The longest field goal in NFL history had been only 56 yards long, and that record had stood for 17 years.

Burkett's snap came back to Scarpati. He placed

35

the ball perfectly and Dempsey really got under it, driving the ball past the outstretched hands of the Detroit defenders. Time on the clock ran out as the ball sailed toward the goal posts. By the time the ball reached the posts, it was so far away Dempsey could hardly make it out.

He didn't have to see it. "I saw the referee's hands go up and everybody started yelling and I knew it was good," he said after his teammates had carried him off the field on their shoulders.

A man with a serious handicap had kicked a last-second field goal to give his team an upset victory. And it was no ordinary kick—it was the longest field goal in NFL history, seven yards longer than the old record!

Dempsey boots the ball from his own 37-yard line. The kick was good, winning the game for the Saints and setting a field goal record—63 yards.

6.
Hurricane Game

On October 26, 1952, the wind howled through Kyle Field in College Station, Texas, and the rain came down in sheets. According to the Weather Bureau, a hurricane was roaring into southeast Texas off the Gulf of Mexico. The worst of the giant storm had not yet reached College Station, which was 100 miles inland— the weather could only get worse. But at the campus of Texas A&M, people's minds were as much on football as on the weather. That afternoon the Aggies were to play their arch-rivals, Texas Christian University.

Texas Christian, with All-America halfback Jim Swink, was rated the fourth-best team in the country. The year before, the Horned Frogs had lost only one game—to A&M. They wanted revenge. The home-town Aggies had won four straight games that season and were hoping to take the Southwest Conference championship away from TCU.

Now the two teams would meet under hurricane conditions. The question was not only what one team could do to another, but what the weather could do to both. More than 42,000 hardy fans came out despite hurricane warnings to see what would happen.

To the dismay of the spectators, they could barely see the players on the field. Then the skies grew darker and the rain came down even harder. When the lightning streaked across the sky, eerie shadows were cast on Kyle Field. The wind was gusting with such strength that the officials had to hold the ball down between plays to keep it from being blown off the field.

The weather was hardest on TCU's strong passing attack. If the wind would blow the ball away when it was on the ground, what would it do to a ball in the air? But the runners didn't have an easy time either. TCU's All-America runner Jim Swink managed to move his team toward the goal in the first half, but whenever he got close, the A&M defense and the weather rose up to stop him. The running game was soon a shoving match in a mud bath. TCU twice got within a few feet of the goal line. A penalty stopped the threat the first time. The second time Swink carried the ball on fourth down for what he—and every TCU supporter in the stadium—thought was a touchdown. But the referee said Swink was stopped short of the end zone, and A&M took over. The first half ended with no score. Fans began to wonder if either team *could* score in these conditions.

While the coaches were discussing second-half strategy with their players, the fans spent the intermission discussing the weather. On Houston Bay, a two-hour trip from the stadium, at least two people had been killed, and dozens of boats had been capsized or reported missing. As the storm moved inland toward College Station, it lost little of its fury. The half-time show at the stadium was canceled.

But the football game continued. The rain stopped in the third quarter, but the field was still a muddy swamp and the wind still whistled. TCU passer Chuck Curtis took advantage of the improved visibility and revved up the Frog passing attack. He took TCU into field goal range twice, but the wind frustrated kicker Vern Hallbeck and both attempts fell short.

Then in the closing moments of the third period, TCU drove deep into A&M territory again. With the ball on the 12-yard line, Curtis dropped back to pass and spotted receiver O'Day Williams in the end zone. Williams brought the pass down with one hand for the first score of the game. The extra-point attempt was wide, but TCU had a 6–0 lead.

At the start of the fourth quarter the weather changed moods once more, taking a turn for the worse. The sky darkened, the winds picked up and the rains came down. Again the passing game seemed impossible, and the running conditions were worse than ever. Even punters weren't safe. With about ten minutes left,

A&M quarterback Randy Osborne tried a quick kick in a third-down-and-long-yardage situation. Before he could get the ball away, he slipped and fell. He got back up and still managed to kick the ball, but a TCU player was there to block it. TCU's Vern Uecker recovered the ball at the A&M 22-yard line.

On the next play TCU's Jim Swink carried the ball to the 17. Then quarterback Chuck Curtis went for the clincher. He fired a pass toward Jim Shofner in the end zone, but the Aggies' Don Watson got there first and made a diving interception.

With nine minutes left to play and trailing 6–0, Texas A&M had a first down on their own 20-yard line. John David Crow (later a standout in the NFL) carried around left end for 21 yards. Quarterback Osborne sneaked through the line for two more. Then Don Watson, who had intercepted the pass only minutes earlier, slithered past the defense for 37 yards. Only a spectacular tackle by a TCU defender at the 20-yard line prevented a touchdown. The Aggies were finally making their running attack work. This was the first time they had gotten inside the TCU 25-yard line.

Relentlessly, they pushed to the TCU 8-yard line. There, quarterback Osborne took the snap and pitched out to Don Watson, who started going wide around end. Watson slowed down, stopped, cocked his arm and threw the ball to John David Crow in the end zone. Touchdown! The Aggies' first pass of the day had tied the score.

Now it was up to A&M place-kicker Loyd Taylor.

No one had made a kick all day, but if his extra-point attempt was good, A&M might well win the game. Hero Don Watson held the ball, and Taylor's kick was good. The drenched crowd and the A&M players, almost unrecognizable in their mud-covered jerseys, jumped up and down in celebration. A one-point lead is a big lead in a hurricane.

A few minutes later, the game ended. TCU had failed to score, and A&M had won the hurricane game, 7–6.

7.
The Littlest Pass

The Little General—leader of the Dallas Cowboys—was getting ready to lead his troops against the Washington Redskins. He was going into battle with revenge on his mind. For seven years he had been quarterback of the Redskins. Now, on October 9, 1960, he was calling signals for the other side—the Dallas Cowboys. Washington had traded him to Dallas, a new expansion team which was fielding its first squad in 1960.

At 5-foot-7 and 167 pounds, Eddie LeBaron—the Little General—was the littlest Cowboy. His size and position as quarterback had earned him his nickname while he was still in Washington, but there was nothing small about his accomplishments. In his seven years in Washington, Eddie had completed nearly half his passes (539 of 1,104 attempts) for 8,068 yards and 59 touchdowns.

The Little General, Eddie LeBaron, in 1952.

LeBaron was returning to the scene of past campaigns and past triumphs. But now he would like nothing better than to show his old team what kind of general he still was.

The Redskin quarterback also had a score to settle. For three years, Ralph Guglielmi had been forced to sit on the Washington bench as LeBaron called the plays. Now that LeBaron had been traded, Guglielmi was finally getting the chance to prove himself. Today he could show everyone his talents in head-to-head combat against the Little General.

For most of the game, LeBaron and Guglielmi played about even. The Little General threw a 32-yard scoring pass in the first period, and Guglielmi had a scoring toss in the second. The big difference in the game was Washington's field goal kicker, rookie Bob Khayat. By the middle of the fourth quarter he had made four field goals, giving the Redskins a hefty 19–7 lead.

Then little Eddie LeBaron rallied his troops, driving the rag-tag Cowboys down the field. Soon he had first down and goal to go on the Washington 1-yard line. In the next few plays he showed his generalship and incidentally managed to set an NFL record. On the first two downs he gave the ball to fullback Don McIlhenny, who smashed into the Redskin line. That moved the ball to within two inches of the goal line. Now it was third down.

When LeBaron came up to the line, the Redskin

defenders were massed on the line, expecting another play through the middle. But the Little General surprised them. He stepped back and threw a short pass to receiver Dick Bielski. Touchdown! That made the score Washington 19, Dallas 14.

LeBaron didn't get his revenge that day. Guglielmi and the Redskins scored again, and the hapless Cowboys didn't. The final score was Redskins 26, Cowboys 14. But when the statistics were released they showed that LeBaron had set one of the NFL's strangest records. Not only had he surprised his former teammates with that scoring pass in the fourth quarter, he had thrown the shortest scoring pass on record—two inches. The old record had been four inches. Somehow it seemed appropriate that the Little General should get into the record book with the littlest touchdown pass ever thrown.

8.
Marathon Man

It is not uncommon for a college athlete to play soccer Saturday morning and then kick field goals for the football team the same afternoon. But the "double-header" that Bill (Dolly) King played for Long Island University was indeed rare.

It was Thanksgiving Day 1939, and Long Island University (LIU) was playing a prominent role in national collegiate sports. The New York basketball team had gone undefeated the previous year. This night the LIU five would try to extend their winning streak to 35 in the first game of the season. All of the previous year's starters had graduated.

The school's football team was also doing well. LIU had dropped football in 1931. Then in 1939 it started a team from scratch as a result of renewed student interest. In this first year, the team, made up completely of sophomores, had won five and lost one. The Thanksgiving Day game against Catholic University of Washington, D.C., would be its last of the season. It was to be played at Ebbets Field, the summer home of baseball's Brooklyn Dodgers.

But LIU had a problem: the star of the football and basketball teams was the same man, Dolly King. He was the left end for the Blackbirds on the gridiron, and the center on the basketball court.

In those days a player usually played the whole game. In football he would play the full 60 minutes—both offense and defense. In basketball, the full 40 minutes was the rule except in cases of injury. It hardly seemed possible that one man could do both in one day.

When the Long Island team lined up for the

Dolly King (right) on the football field.

kickoff at Ebbets Field, Dolly King was there. He played sixty minutes as left end—offensive and defensive. Late in the second quarter LIU was down, 14–0. Then Dolly caught a 32-yard pass and a 5-yard touchdown pass to put LIU back in the game. The score at half time was 14–7.

In the second half Dolly played good defense and caught some more passes, but LIU was overpowered by the stronger Catholic University squad. The final score was 35–14. It was hardly a good way to end the season, but Dolly King had played a fine game. Sportswriters later suggested that Dolly might have become an All-America end if he had played for a nationally-ranked eleven.

He was, however, playing for a nationally-ranked basketball team, coached by the famous Clair Bee. A loss in football in the afternoon was one thing. A basketball defeat that night just wouldn't do. Dolly would have to play center that night for the Blackbirds.

And play he did. The game was against the LIU alumni, which included some of the players from last season's unbeaten team. Dolly scored only one basket, but he went up and down the court for the entire 40-minute game. He rebounded as though he had been resting up all day. The varsity won that night, 59–41, and extended its winning streak. LIU would win 42 straight before losing. With Dolly King leading the way, the quintet wound up with a 20–3 season.

The Iron Man of LIU athletics went on to a profes-

King gets set to play basketball.

sional basketball career, then became a college referee
and coach. His teams at Manhattan Community College had won 50 games and lost only 7 when Dolly
died suddenly in January 1969.

The newspaper obituaries exaggerated Dolly's
Thanksgiving Day accomplishment. They said he was
the high scorer in both the football and basketball
games that day. But no matter, Dolly's feat had established him as his school's Rock of Gibraltar.

50

9.
Scoreboard Trouble

The world of minor league professional football is not a glamorous one. For the player it means working all day at a regular job and practicing at night, often waiting until a high school team is finished with the field.

The road trips, usually in a rented school bus, are long and hard, and the pay is poor—almost nothing compared to players' salaries in the National Football League. Most of the minor league players know they will never reach the NFL. In fact, many have had tryouts and failed to make the grade. Others are just former college athletes who would rather play football on weekends than almost anything else.

Every now and then there is a moment, or a game, which makes up for all the trouble and difficulties of playing in the minors. One such game took place on September 2, 1967.

The Richmond Mustangs were playing host to the Savannah Indians in a United-American Professional Football League game. The Richmond team had won its first two games by scores of 40–0 and 73–0. But they didn't know what to expect from Savannah.

It was a warm Labor Day weekend, and the Richmond Braves of the International League were playing a home baseball game the same night. Yet more than 6,400 fans came to Richmond City Stadium to see the Mustangs—a good crowd for minor league football.

The Richmond players began to worry with seven minutes gone in the first quarter. They hadn't been able to do much against the Savannah defense. Apparently the visiting Indians had not read about those big scores the Mustangs had rolled up in their first two games. The Richmond fans were restless, too. But then Richmond quarterback Marv Holland flipped a twelve-yard pass to Jake Adams for a Richmond touchdown.

Now the fun began. Before the first period was over, Holland connected on passes of 13 and 32 yards to Broaddus Cox to make the score 21–0. The Mustangs ran wild in the second quarter, scoring on runs, passes, recovered fumbles and a pass interception. Richmond scored five more touchdowns in the period, and the score at half time was Richmond 56, Savannah 0.

There was no letup in the third quarter as Richmond linebacker Don Christman intercepted his second pass of the game and returned it for a touchdown. Second-string quarterback Don Redford threw a couple of scoring passes. The Mustangs scored four more touchdowns, and the scoreboard began to look like a computer as the score reached 84–0.

The happy Richmond fans stayed glued to their seats, waiting to see how high the score would go. With five minutes and 50 seconds remaining, quarterback Redford hit Jake Adams with a five-yard TD pass and the scoreboard couldn't tell the right score anymore. It read: Home 05, Visitors 0. Richmond had passed the 100-point mark.

It wasn't all offense for the home team, though. The Mustang defense allowed Savannah only three first downs. Late in the third period, the Indians had advanced the ball to Richmond's 48-yard line—their deepest penetration—but were thrown for a ten-yard loss on the next play. On the play after that, Richmond intercepted a desperation pass to end the Savannah "threat."

The crowd was hoping for more offense, though, even after the 100-point mark was reached. But Richmond fumbled on the 4-yard line with three minutes remaining, and the fans began to file out. Savannah was able to run out the clock and avoid another score. The final count: Richmond 105, Savannah 0.

Richmond coach Dick James couldn't be accused

of running up the score deliberately. After the game he said, "I played everybody on the bench and had them shuttling in and out all through the second half."

James, who was something of an inspiration to his players since he had been an NFL star with the Washington Redskins, even paid the Savannah team a compliment. "Why, Savannah was the hardest-hitting team we've met," he said.

10.
Breaks of the Game

A football player expects to hit and be hit on almost every play. He worries and sweats to get into top condition so that he can take the beating he knows he will receive. A coach worries and sweats, too, but he doesn't expect to take a physical beating. He stays off the field and works in the "non-contact" side of the sport. But sometimes the unexpected happens, as coach Dan Devine would be the first to admit.

Devine was in his first year as coach of the Green Bay Packers. It was 1971, and the New York Giants had come to Green Bay for the first game of the season. It was supposed to be the easiest game on the Packer schedule.

But the first three quarters had been a disaster. In the first half New York had scored four touchdowns.

The Packers' Doug Hart intercepts a pass and heads for the sidelines near the Green Bay bench.

Two of them had been giveaways. Twice Packer Dave Hampton fumbled in his own end zone, and twice the Giants recovered for easy touchdowns. The Packers lost more ground in the third quarter. Going into the final period, the Giants had a big 42–24 lead.

But then the Packers caught fire. Rookie quarterback Scott Hunter moved the team from the Packer 27-yard line into Giant territory. Fullback Donny Anderson carried the ball in for a touchdown on a 19-yard play. Now the Packers trailed by eleven points, 42–31. The Green Bay fans sensed that the Pack could still come back. But they would have to hurry—the

Giants had the ball and the Packers needed two more touchdowns.

Giant quarterback Fran Tarkenton moved New York to a first down. Now there were only seven minutes left. Devine knew that Tarkenton would be taking his time. If the Packers wanted a chance to win they would have to take the ball away from the Giants.

Devine's hopes were realized on the very next play —a play that he would never forget. Tarkenton threw a pass and Packer Doug Hart intercepted it near the sidelines on the Packer side of the field. Giant Bob Hyland charged at Hart, trying to knock him out of bounds. But Hyland slipped on the wet turf and ran into the wrong man: Dan Devine. The coach was watching the play intently and not expecting to be a part of it. He went down hard. So hard, in fact, that he broke his leg. The injury was soon diagnosed by the team doctor, and Devine was carried to the locker room on a stretcher, on his way to the hospital.

The Packers determined to try and win the game for their injured coach. With four minutes left, quarterback Scott Hunter passed for a touchdown to bring the Packers within four points of the Giants.

The Packer defense held, and with two minutes left the Giants went into punt formation. The snap from

Packer coach Dan Devine is carried off the field after being hit by a Giant tackler.

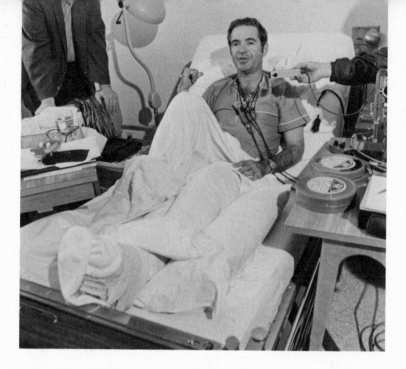

In the hospital Devine watches films of the game—including the play in which he was tackled by mistake.

center went sailing over the punter's head, and a Packer recovered the ball in the end zone for a safety. Now Green Bay was behind by only two points, 42–40, and the Giants had to kick off. The Packers were still hoping to get the win for coach Devine.

On the next set of downs, Hunter moved the Packers to the Giant 36-yard line. But then, with time running out, he threw an interception. The Giants ran out the clock and held on to their victory.

So the day was a double loss to Dan Devine. Not only had his team gone down to defeat, but he had ended up in the hospital.

No doubt he muttered something about the breaks of the game.

11.
Sooner or Later

It was forecast as a great day for the state of Oklahoma. November 16, 1957. The state was celebrating its 50th birthday. And the University of Oklahoma was playing football against Notre Dame. Everyone expected Oklahoma's Sooners to win. There was hardly a student at the university who remembered Oklahoma losing—they had won 47 straight games. A victory today would tie the record for the longest college winning streak in history. Another of Oklahoma's records was almost as amazing: the team had scored in every game for nearly twelve seasons—123 straight games.

One of the biggest reasons for the Sooners' success on the gridiron was their coach, Bud Wilkinson. His record going into the Notre Dame game was 101 victo-

Coach Bud Wilkinson (standing) encourages his Oklahoma players during their record-setting winning streak.

ries, eight losses and three ties. In the previous two seasons the Sooners had been national champions. This year they were ranked second in the polls with a 7–0 record.

Oklahoma was rated an 18-point favorite over Notre Dame's Fighting Irish. The year before, they had trounced the Irish 40–0. Just a week before the game Oklahoma had beat Missouri, 34–14, while Notre Dame had been whipped by Michigan State, 34–6. It seemed certain that the game would be one-sided. Yet because of the Sooners' winning streak and the state's birthday, the game was being shown on national television.

When the game started, Oklahoma was on the attack. On their very first series of plays they drove 45 yards from their own 38. When they lost the ball on downs at the Notre Dame 13-yard line, their fans told each other that the team was just warming up. Then with six minutes left in the first quarter, the Sooners recovered a Notre Dame fumble on the Irish 34. This was the kind of chance Oklahoma seldom muffed. But the surprisingly rugged Irish defense held, and the Sooners failed again. They seemed slow to warm up today, the fans were saying.

As the quarter ended, Wilkinson's crew had threatened again, driving to the Notre Dame 23. But on the first play of the second period, Oklahoma's Carl Dodd fumbled. Someone booted the ball by mistake, and it rolled almost to midfield before Notre Dame's Nick

Notre Dame's Nick Pietrosante (49) is stopped by Oklahoma after a short gain.

Pietrosante recovered. Another bad break for the Sooners. A few of the home fans began to worry. But then Notre Dame had not scored either.

The Irish were on the move, however. Following the fumble recovery, quarterback Bob Williams took his team all the way to Oklahoma's 3-yard line. First down and goal to go. Now the home team was really in trouble.

Williams handed to Pietrosante, his fullback, on the next two downs. Nick went a yard on each—down to the one-yard line. The next hand-off went to Frank Reynolds, who took the ball to the one-foot line. Could Oklahoma hold one more time? The ball went to Jim Just and he was stopped cold. Oklahoma took possession. It had been a close call.

The very next time Notre Dame got the ball they threatened again. They seemed to be stopped with fourth down on the 16-yard line and went into field goal formation. It was a fake! Bob Williams passed to Just, complete on the six. First and goal. Two plays later Williams threw again—into the end zone. Oklahoma's Dave Baker made a desperate, lunging stab—and intercepted the ball! Oklahoma had held again.

The Oklahoma defense needed their rest at half time. Who ever expected the intermission score to read 0–0? People were starting to wonder if the game was a birthday surprise. If it was, it wasn't a very happy one for Oklahoma.

In the second half, Oklahoma was stopped again and again. Notre Dame couldn't manage to score, but they were still managing to move the ball. Oklahoma fans still had one big hope left. The Sooners were famous for their fourth-quarter drives. Today they would really need one. But as the game neared its end, it was still 0–0.

Then, late in the fourth quarter, Notre Dame got the ball at its own 20-yard line following a touchback. This would likely be the Fighting Irish's last chance to score. Then if they couldn't, the Sooners would have a final chance to show their last-quarter heroics.

Play after play, the Notre Dame offense picked up short yardage. Fullback Pietrosante and halfback Dick Lynch bulled through time and again. The Irish marched 72 yards. Now it was first and goal at the

**Dick Lynch sweeps right end and goes into the end zone for a
Notre Dame touchdown.**

Oklahoma 8-yard line. Again, the Oklahoma defense
was up against the wall. On first down Pietrosante
crashed through the middle for four yards. On second
down the Sooners held, and Lynch was stopped without a gain. Third and goal from the 4. Quarterback
Williams tried to carry through the center himself, but
picked up only one more yard. That made it fourth
down and goal to go from the 3-yard line. The Notre
Dame coach decided to go for the touchdown, not the
field goal.

The crowd was on its feet. How would the Irish try
to score? Could Oklahoma hold again? The ball was
snapped. Pietrosante headed off-tackle, and Williams
faked a hand-off to him. The quarterback then pitched
to Lynch, who was sweeping around right end. He

Returning home after the great upset, the Notre Dame team is
greeted with cheers and banners.

scampered into the end zone standing up! The Irish were ahead!

Oklahoma took the ball on the kickoff and started a last-ditch drive. But time was too short, even for a great fourth-quarter team. A Notre Dame defenseman intercepted a desperation pass. A few moments later the gun sounded and the birthday party was over. So were the winning streak and the scoring streak.

Final score: Notre Dame 7, Oklahoma 0. Oklahomans couldn't believe it. On opening day in 1953 the Sooners had lost—to Notre Dame. Now, nearly five full seasons later, they had lost again—to Notre Dame. Of course, 47 straight victories was nothing to be ashamed of—no major college team has approached that record since. And it may be that none ever will.

12.

Lost Down

The scene is the Los Angeles Coliseum, Sunday, December 8, 1968. The Los Angeles Rams have a 10-1-1 record, but are still striving to stay in contention with the Baltimore Colts for the Coastal Division championship of the National Football League. The Colts have a 12–1 record, so Los Angeles needs a victory or it will be mathematically eliminated for the championship.

The Rams' opponents are the Chicago Bears, with a mediocre 6–6 record, but still good enough for a first-place tie in the NFL's Central Division. The Bears need a victory in order to keep their own title hopes alive.

The Bears are 14-point underdogs going into the game. Yet they strike quickly, taking the opening kickoff and marching deep into Ram territory before being stopped. Mac Percival kicks a 20-yard field goal, giving Chicago a 3–0 lead.

Chicago's defense, built around middle linebacker Dick Butkus, blocks the Los Angeles offense until the second quarter when the Rams recover a fumble by Chicago's Ronnie Bull and drive 40 yards for a touchdown.

On the kickoff, Dick Butkus picks up the ball and flips it to Clarence Childs. Childs rambles through the Ram defenders for 88 yards before being brought down on the Los Angeles 2-yard line. Running back Brian Piccolo dives over on the next play, and the Bears take the lead again, 10–7.

Early in the third quarter the Bears get a big break—again provided by Dick Butkus. The big linebacker intercepts a pass on the Los Angeles 32-yard line. Chicago drives to the Los Angeles goal, scoring on a four-yard rollout pass. The Rams score a safety when a blocked Chicago punt rolls out of the end zone. But at the end of the third quarter, they still trail 17–9.

With only two minutes gone in the final period, the Rams are knocking on the door. With the ball on the Chicago 9-yard line, running back Tommy Mason carries into the line. He is met by the Bears' Dick Evey with such impact that the ball bounces loose. Dick Butkus is there to recover.

The Rams' defensive standouts Merlin Olsen and Deacon Jones have been weakened by the flu, but now the defenders hold on and the Bears are forced to punt.

Time is running out for the Ram offense. Ram quarterback Roman Gabriel, who has been having one of his worst days as a pro, drives his team into Bear territory but stalls at the Bear 27-yard line. Bruce Gossett is called in to attempt the field goal. In four of the ten Ram victories this season, Gossett's foot has provided the winning margin. But this time Gossett's kick goes wide and the Rams still trail 17–9. It appears that they are not going to win today, that the championship is not going to be theirs this year.

With the ball on their own 20 after the missed field goal, the Bears try to use up as much time as possible by running plays through the middle. They make one first down but on the next series they miss on third down. As Jon Kilgore goes back to punt, only four minutes of play remain. At the snap of the ball, the Ram rushers charge at Kilgore. Willie Daniel breaks through and deflects the kick. The ball bounces crazily toward the Bear goal line. Finally, Ram Doug Woodlief falls on it on the Bears' 16-yard line.

Suddenly there is hope for the Rams. On the fourth play from scrimmage Gabriel rolls out and completes a pass in the end zone. The point-after is good, and the Rams trail 17–16. The time remaining: two minutes and 42 seconds.

Once again the Rams kick off to the Bears, who try to run out the clock. Los Angeles calls time out every chance it has, hoping for another opportunity to score. The Bears fail to make a first down and punt deep into Los Angeles territory. The Rams put the ball into play on their own 23 with one minute left in the game.

Everyone in the Coliseum—especially the Bears—knows the Rams will come out passing. They have no time-outs remaining. Gabriel's first attempt to split end Jack Snow is incomplete. Then Gabriel hits Mike Dennis for a 13-yard gain and a first down on the Los Angeles 36. He throws twice more incomplete and then connects with Jack Snow for a 32-yard gain. The Rams are now on the Bear 32-yard line, within field goal range. It is first down, and there is a half a minute of playing time remaining.

On first down Gabriel passes to Snow, incomplete. But Ram lineman Charley Cowan is detected holding. The Bears accept the penalty, which costs the Rams 21 yards since it is measured from the point of the infraction—six yards behind the line of scrimmage.

So the Rams start over. It is first down and 31 yards to go back on their own 47-yard line.

At least it is supposed to be first down. But for some reason, the official marker on the sidelines tells everyone in the stadium that it is second down. The big number "2" is there for all to see. Los Angeles Coach George Allen is watching the clock, and Ram quarterback Roman Gabriel is busy calling plays. No one notices the big number "2." Gabriel throws three more incomplete passes. He still should have a fourth down try, but he trots off the field as referee Norm Schacter signals "first and 10" for the Chicago Bears. There are five seconds on the clock. Concannon takes the snap from center, falls on the ball and the game is over. The Bears have won, 17–16.

But that isn't the end of the story.

Newspaper reporters in the press box and millions of fans who watched the nationally televised game all knew that the Rams were cheated out of a down. In this game situation, the lost down may well have cost the Rams the game. With one throw left, it is quite possible that Gabriel would have hit the jackpot, winning the game and perhaps taking the Rams into the playoffs.

The amazing thing was that no one on the field noticed the lost down. Coach George Allen of the Rams was one of the shrewdest men in football—he missed it. So did the Rams on the bench and those on the field.

The league was amazed that the officials made the mistake in the first place. Days later, after viewing game films and reading the official play-by-play chart of the game, the league officially decided that the Rams should have had one more chance. In a move unprecedented in college or professional football, the league suspended the officials without pay.

But league action couldn't make good what might have been. The Rams still lost the game—and a chance at the championship.

13.
Snow Champs

It was Sunday, December 19, 1948. The kids in Philadelphia were delighted. Snow covered the ground—and kept drifting down. The temperature was below freezing and the weatherman predicted accumulations of up to two feet—a real blizzard. Christmas was only six days away, and it certainly was going to be a white Christmas.

At Shibe Park, though, it was a different story. At 1:30 that afternoon National Football League's championship game was supposed to begin. Commissioner Bert Bell could hardly see the field through the falling flakes. Football games are hardly ever canceled, but Bell was thinking that perhaps this one should be.

The hometown Philadelphia Eagles were scheduled to meet the defending champion Chicago Cardi-

Eagle and Cardinal players help remove the snow-covered tarpaulin from the field so that the game can begin.

nals. They had met before in the 1947 NFL title game and the Cardinals had won, 28–21. Philadelphia fans were looking forward to this chance to get even. But now the question was: would the weather defeat both teams?

Jim Conzelman, the vice president and coach of

the Cardinals, said that his team was ready to play and couldn't see any reason for postponing the game. After all, the conditions would be the same for both teams, he said.

Earle (Greasy) Neale, coach of the Eagles, wanted a postponement. He said it was foolish to work toward a championship all season and then have it decided partly by the weather. But if the Cardinals insisted on playing, Neale said, the Eagles would be ready.

Commissioner Bell made the final decision: the game would go on.

At 1:30, when the players were supposed to be lining up for the kickoff, they were busy helping the grounds crew roll up the tarpaulin which had covered the field all week. Now it was covered with a heavy blanket of snow, making the job difficult and time-consuming. As soon as the tarp was up, however, a whole new set of problems was revealed. The chalk used to mark the yards and sidelines had stuck to the tarpaulin. The field was an unmarked expanse of brown-green grass rapidly being covered with snow.

Commissioner Bell ordered some adjustments. The 10-yard chains would be used to mark first downs, but there would be no measuring. The referee would be the final judge of all first downs. Ropes were hurriedly stretched up and down the field and fastened to stakes to mark the sidelines.

The lights were turned on, lighting the falling snow as well as the football players, who looked like ghosts moving about in the swirling flakes. More than 33,000 tickets had been sold for the game, and only about 4,500 fans stayed home. The rest were in the stands when the teams lined up for the opening kickoff at about 2 o'clock.

Chicago took the kickoff. The weather discouraged passing, so the Cardinals gave the ball to their runners, Charley Trippi and Elmer Angsman. But enough snow had fallen on the field to make the going slippery. After three downs Chicago was forced to punt.

Philadelphia put the ball in play on its own 37-yard line. The Eagle quarterback was Tommy Thompson, who had completed 27 of 44 passes in the 1947 title game. He would not match that performance today. But on the first play from scrimmage, hoping to surprise the Cardinals, Thompson faded back to pass and threw a long one to Jack Ferrante on the Chicago 20-yard line.

As he caught the pass Ferrante was being charged by two Chicago defenders. But the field was as slippery for the defense as for the offense—they slid past him on the slick field. He ran into the end zone untouched. The Eagles had worked on that play for ten days, hoping to take an early lead over the Cardinals.

The effort was all in vain. The officials had noticed that Ferrante had been a little too anxious to get downfield on the play and had been offside. The play was called back, and the Eagles had to start again from their own 30-yard line. This time they didn't get very far in the snow.

Now the Cardinals tried their luck again. Elmer Angsman did most of the ball-carrying, including a 28-yard gainer which put the ball on the Eagle 30-yard line. But then the Eagle defense held. On fourth down Cardinal Pat Harder was called in to try a field goal from 37 yards out. The Chicago players got down on their hands and knees and cleared the snow away from the spot where the ball would be placed down. The goal posts were barely visible. Harder's kick sailed wide of the mark, and the score remained 0–0.

The two teams pushed each other around on the treacherous field for the rest of the first half. The ball was cold and slippery and visibility was poor, so passing was limited. The footing was so bad that ball-carriers couldn't turn a corner, ruling out end runs—only one runner was forced out of bounds during the first half. The Eagles had driven deep into Chicago territory once. But kicker Cliff Patton missed a field goal attempt.

The Eagles mounted another drive midway through the third quarter, but Patton missed another fourth-down field goal try. With the uncertain footing, the thick snow flurries and gusting wind, it was not a good day for place-kickers.

Late in the third period, the Cardinals' Elmer Angsman fumbled and Philadelphia recovered on the Cardinal 17-yard line. Now the Eagles had an instant scoring threat. Eagle ball-carrier Bosh Pritchard slipped and slid to the 11-yard line on the last play of the third quarter.

77

When the teams changed ends of the field, they
started play on virgin snow. The snow had been falling
so fast that footprints from earlier plays had already
been covered.

It was second down, five yards to go, on the Chicago 11. Joe Muha carried for three. Then quarterback Thompson kept it himself, going for three more
yards and a first down. With the ball on the 5-yard
line, Thompson called Steve Van Buren's number, and
the burly back headed between left guard and tackle
and straight for the end zone. Touchdown.

Philadelphia's Steve Van Buren carries the ball across the goal for the only score of the afternoon.

The Eagles cleared a patch of ground where the ball could be placed for the extra-point attempt. Cliff Patton's kick was good, and Philadelphia went ahead 7–0.

The Cardinals tried desperately to come back. But the Eagles played cautiously, taking particular care not to lose the ball in their own territory. By now the players on both sides were numb with the cold. When the gun sounded, the score was still 7–0. The Eagles had gotten even with Chicago—with a little help from the Blizzard of '48.

14.
Last Man

Coaches like to emphasize the importance of team-work in football. They pepper their players with slogans like "Football is an eleven-man game," and "Every man counts."

No coach could offer a more dramatic example of the truth of these slogans than Dutch Meyer of Texas Christian University in Fort Worth, Texas.

It was during the 1923 season when Dutch was coaching the freshman team. In those days the squads were very small, often with fewer than 20 boys on the team. The schools scrimped and saved on expenses every way they could. As a result, freshman teams usually found themselves playing mostly against local high schools.

One big game for the TCU freshmen each year was

Texas Christian's long-time football coach, Dutch Meyer.

against Terrell Prep in nearby Dallas. The games were usually hard-fought and close, but in 1923 the TCU freshmen were clearly superior. They began scoring early and held the poor Terrell Prep team scoreless.

The rules in those days restricted substitutions. When a player was taken out, he couldn't return to action until the following quarter. The rule didn't worry coach Meyer since eleven men usually played the whole game. But then a couple of the TCU regulars were injured early in the game, so Meyer began to send in his substitutes—he had only five. Soon he was using almost every able-bodied player on the squad.

Then in the fourth quarter, with the TCU frosh ahead 63–0, TCU got into substitution trouble that almost cost the team the game.

"Out on the field, one of our boys took a swing at an opponent and was put out of the game," Meyer later related. "I looked up and down the bench, but every boy shook his head." All of them had either been taken out during the quarter or were unable to play because of injuries.

"I had put my last eligible substitute into the game," Meyer continued. "There I was with only ten men on the field. The referee was reminding me that the rules say there shall be eleven players on each team. It looked like the game would have to be forfeited."

There were only two or three plays left in the game, and the coach certainly didn't want to forfeit.

Just then, Ernest Lowry, who had been injured on the opening kickoff, struggled up off a blanket and mumbled to Meyer, "I'm eligible, coach. I'm all right. I'll go in."

The effort to sit up, though, caused the boy to pass out. Then the desperate coach had a brainstorm. He placed Lowry's blanket on the field just in-bounds, and the injured player was laid on it. He was far from the action, but he was a legal eleventh man.

"We were on defense," Meyer explained, "so he could be any place back of the line of scrimmage. And he lay there during the final plays of the game. He gave us our eleventh man. It's the only time an unconscious man ever won a football game."

15.
Bombs Away

Joe Namath was no favorite of Baltimore Colt fans. Before Super Bowl III, in January 1969, "Broadway Joe" had laughed at the experts who said the Colts would whip his New York Jets. "We're going to win," he boasted. "Bet on it."

Then Joe had gone out and made good on his prediction, leading the Jets to a shocking 16–7 upset of the Colts.

In the years since that game, the Jets and the Colts had met many times. But Namath had never appeared in Baltimore. Every time the Jets went to play there, Joe had been injured and the Jets had been forced to use another quarterback.

Then on September 24, 1972, Namath made his first appearance in Baltimore since the Super Bowl.

When his name was announced in the starting line-up, boos filled Memorial Stadium. The Baltimore fans hadn't forgotten, and they wanted to see Namath beaten.

The quarterback for Baltimore was Johnny Unitas, who was completing his 17-year career with the Colts. Johnny had won his first championship for the team in 1958. He had gone on to lead the Colts to one winning season after another, compiling passing records that fill the record books. Now he was nearing retirement. If Joe Namath was the villain in Baltimore, Johnny Unitas was the hero.

When Unitas was winning his early championships, one of his fans had been a kid in Beaver Falls, Pennsylvania, who was a quarterback, too. This young man patterned himself after Unitas and became a star of Beaver Falls High, the University of Alabama—and finally the New York Jets. His name, of course, was Joe Namath. Today he would be facing his old hero, perhaps for the final time. This would be one last chance for the two quarterbacks to prove who was best.

Shortly after the game started, the Jets had the ball on their own 37-yard line. Namath went back to pass and threw to little receiver Ed Bell, who took the ball all the way into the end zone. One touchdown for Joe —on a 63-yard play.

Moments later, Unitas called the famous Baltimore "flea-flicker" play. He handed the ball to halfback Tom Matte, who was heading around end. But at the

Joe Namath throws to John Riggins on a 67-yard scoring play late in the second quarter.

last moment, Matte lateraled the ball back to Unitas, who threw it to receiver Sam Havrilak for a touchdown. The Jets had been expecting the play and had worked on it in practice. But in the game they were caught flat-footed. One touchdown for Unitas.

Then the game settled down, becoming a defensive battle until late in the second quarter. The Colts had scored on two field goals and led 13–7. But their lead against Namath's Jets was precarious, as the next few minutes would show.

First Namath and running back John Riggins teamed up on a 67-yard scoring pass, putting New York ahead 14–13. The Jets' kickoff was grabbed by Don McCauley, who scrambled 93 yards for a Baltimore touchdown. Colts 20, Jets 14. The Jets drove rapidly down the field and scored when Namath hit Don Maynard with a 28-yard scoring toss to go ahead again. Baltimore took the kickoff. Then on the first play from scrimmage Unitas fumbled. New York recovered, and on its first play Namath passed to Rich Caster, who was alone in the end zone. In 89 seconds Namath had thrown three touchdown passes and the Jets had taken a 27–20 lead.

The second half started slowly. The only scoring in the entire third quarter was a 14-yard field goal by New York's Bobby Howfield, giving the Jets a ten-point lead at 30–20.

Although Baltimore did not have wide receivers as fast or as dangerous as the Jets', Johnny Unitas was a master of the long touchdown drive. His short passes to halfback Tom Matte and tight end Tom Mitchell moved Baltimore toward a score early in the fourth quarter. Finally Don McCauley scored on a one-yard plunge. New York 30, Baltimore 27.

The Jets returned the kickoff to their own 21-yard line. Then on the first play from scrimmage, Namath cranked up and rifled a pass to his swift tight end, Rich Caster. The 6-foot-5 Caster broke a tackle and sped all the way to pay dirt.

Now Baltimore was behind by ten points and time was running out. Unitas knew what he had to do: score as soon as possible. He marched the Colts downfield, then hit Matte on a swing pass from the Jets' 22-yard line. The halfback carried it into the end zone to narrow New York's lead to three points.

Starting from their own 20-yard line, the Jets were in control—all they had to do was play conservatively, running time-consuming plays on the ground to use up the remaining time and keep Baltimore from scoring again. But on first down, Namath dropped back to pass. He found Caster alone near the left sideline. Caster loped down the field for his third touchdown, completing an 80-yard pass play that was almost an instant replay of the last Jet touchdown.

The score was New York 44, Baltimore 34, and that's the way the game ended. Unitas had completed an amazing 26 of 45 passes for 376 yards, the best performance of his 17-year career.

But the kid from Beaver Falls had an even more spectacular day. Joe Namath threw only 28 passes and completed only 15. But those completions gained 496 yards for an average of 33 yards apiece. Six of the passes went for touchdowns—four of them covering 60 yards or more.

It was the greatest passing day in recent memory. But it was a sad day for Baltimore fans: the villain had won.

16.
Completed Pass

Some players get their names into the record books for many seasons of great play. Only a few quarterbacks have gained over 30,000 yards passing, for example. Others have records from one season's accomplishments or one outstanding game. Norm Van Brocklin, for instance, holds the record for yards gained passing in one game—554.

But there are a few men who get into the record books for what they did in a single play. Quarterback Milt Plum holds one of these records—one of the strangest in the book.

On October 18, 1959, Plum was calling the signals for the Cleveland Browns in a game against the Chicago Cardinals. It had been a dull game, but Cleveland was ahead 17–0 in the second half. Plum had thrown one touchdown pass.

The Browns and the Cardinals were trading punts, neither team being able to move the ball. Then Cleveland got the ball and gained five yards on two plays. It was third down, five to go. Fans groaned. No doubt the Browns would run one more play and then have to punt again, they thought.

The ball was snapped to Plum. He dropped back to pass but was being rushed hard by the Cardinal defenders. He finally threw the ball toward a receiver on the left sideline, but an onrushing Cardinal stuck his hand up and batted the ball—back toward Plum.

The startled quarterback grabbed the ball out of the air and began to run downfield. He picked up 20 yards before he was tackled. First down on a completed pass: Milt Plum to Milt Plum.

A few minutes later the game ended. The Browns had won 17–7. Plum's "special" pass hadn't even figured in the scoring. But it got his name in the record book for a feat that will not easily be duplicated: Longest Reception of Own Pass, 20 Yards.

17.
Flying Success

"What, let my team fly to a football game? Never!"
The speaker was University of New Mexico coach Roy
Johnson. He was talking to sportswriters from the Albuquerque newspapers about an invitation to play Occidental College in California.

Today, football teams fly all the time. But Roy
Johnson was talking in 1929. Only two years before,
Charles Lindbergh had made the first solo flight across
the Atlantic. There were no airlines as we know them
now and, of course, the jet engine had not yet been invented. If Johnson's New Mexico team flew to California, they would fly in rickety planes that held only
eleven passengers. No wonder he said no. No college
team had ever flown to a football game before, the
coach said, and he didn't want his Lobos to be the first.

FLYING SUCCESS

The town of Albuquerque, which then had about 15,000 people, was in the midst of "air fever." Situated in the middle of the Great Southwest, the little city was hundreds of miles from any major population centers. So adventurous citizens began traveling by plane rather than spending dozens of hours on trains or driving for days on hazardous roads. Transcontinental Air Transport, known as T.A.T., was an early flying organization founded by Charles Lindbergh himself. T.A.T. advertised flights across the United States, but they were not really transcontinental, since the passengers flew only during the daylight hours, then traveled in trains after dark. Still, the coast-to-coast trip took *only* 48 hours.

The last leg of the coast-to-coast flight was from Albuquerque to Los Angeles. T.A.T. had suggested to Roy Johnson that the University of New Mexico football team fly to their game to help promote air travel. The trip would take 26 hours by train, they said. By plane it would take only eight. But still Johnson said no.

The people of Albuquerque were upset by his refusal. Some even demanded that the team be allowed to fly. Finally, five days before the game, Johnson yielded to public pressure and said the Lobos would become the first team to fly to a football game.

Johnson made two conditions. First, each player had to bring a note from his parents giving permission for the flight. Secondly, only the substitutes and as-

The University of New Mexico football team poses in front of the Ford Tri-Motor that would carry them to California.

sistant coaches would fly to the game while the first-string players would take the train. On the way back the first-string players could fly. If there were any delays or accidents on the way to California, at least the regular players would arrive safely by train. There were only six seats available on the regular plane from Albuquerque to Los Angeles. And when the airline added another plane, this provided only 11 more seats. So there was no way that the entire 30-man team could fly together anyway.

The 14 first-string players boarded the train at 3:45 A.M. on Thursday. They would arrive in Pasadena

(near Los Angeles) early Friday morning, the day of the game. The rest of the team took off by plane shortly after 10 A.M. Thursday and were in their hotel rooms in Pasadena before sundown. They even had a chance to work out under the floodlights in the new Rose Bowl, where the game would be played Friday night. Night football was also new to the Lobos. Their field in Albuquerque had only recently been planted with grass, and it certainly was not equipped with electric lights.

The huge Rose Bowl, which could hold 100,000 fans, was hardly filled for the game. The crowd was estimated at 17,000, however, more than the entire population of Albuquerque. The New Mexico starters were tired from their long train trip. In addition, they had never played before an audience of this size and had never played at night under the lights.

Occidental opened the scoring in the first quarter. Halfback Glenn Rozelle returned a punt to the New Mexico 30-yard line. Four plays later he bulled into the end zone and then kicked the extra point. The teams were using a white football, thinking that it would be easier to see at night. But the Occidental players were wearing white home uniforms, and the New Mexico players found it almost impossible to detect the white ball against the white jerseys.

New Mexico, perhaps inspired by the plane flight, used an aerial attack, but not very successfully. At the half, they had fallen behind by 13–0.

The half-time show was a spectacular fireworks display featuring a giant sign reading "Welcome Lobos" and a Lobo (wolf) which wagged its fiery tail and spewed flames from its mouth.

Perhaps the New Mexico players were dazzled by the light show during the intermission. Whatever the reason, they were held scoreless again in the second half and lost 26–0.

The next morning the Lobo regulars boarded a T.A.T. plane and flew back to Albuquerque. The second team had been the first to fly to a football game— now the regulars were the first to fly home. Although the trip was a football failure, it was a flying success and a flying first for the Lobos of New Mexico.

18.
Golden Boy

Paul Hornung dressed slowly in the Green Bay locker room. His face showed concern. He was wondering whether he would play at all today against the Baltimore Colts. The week before, he had sat on the bench the entire game.

Five years earlier, in 1960, Paul Hornung had set a National Football League record by scoring 176 points—90 on touchdowns and 86 on extra-point and field-goal kicks. As the top running back and kicker for the Green Bay Packers, he became the toast of the football world.

Called "Golden Boy" because of his blond, curly hair and his engaging manner, Hornung was the Joe Namath of his day. His off-the-field activities were often in the newspapers: romances, parties and attention-getting comments.

But since 1960 his career had gone downhill. The next two seasons the Packers won the NFL championship, but Hornung got fewer chances to carry the ball. In 1962 he was replaced as kicker. Then in April of 1963 he was suspended from league play for at least one season for placing bets on the Packers. When he returned in 1964 he was a starter and place-kicker once again, but things were not the same.

Now it was December 12, 1965. The Packers were facing the Baltimore Colts in a crucial late-season game. Hornung had scored only one touchdown all year. What could he do today?

When the starting line-ups were introduced, Hornung was in the backfield. At fullback was the Packers' other star rusher, Jim Taylor. And at quarterback was Bart Starr. This was the Packer line-up that had won championships. Today they trailed Baltimore by half a game. If the Packers could win, they would be on their way to still another championship and the Golden Boy might regain some of his luster.

The Packers got off to a bad start when the Colts intercepted a Bart Starr pass and quickly scored a field goal. But the next time they got the ball Hornung and Taylor began grinding out yardage on the ground. The Pack moved 80 yards in six plays, and Hornung carried the ball over from the 2-yard line for the touchdown.

Paul Hornung (5) spins into the end zone for a score.

Later in the quarter Green Bay recovered a Baltimore fumble on its own 41. Two plays picked up short yardage. It was third down and two yards to go. Starr faked a handoff to Taylor, who was driving into the line. The defenders pulled in to stop him. Meanwhile, Hornung had slipped out of the backfield and behind the defense, and he was all alone. Starr fired the ball, and Hornung took it into the end zone for his second touchdown of the day. Now it was 14–3, Packers.

The Colts, playing like the division leaders they were, came right back with another field goal and a touchdown by Lenny Moore to make the score 14–13. Then with less than a minute to go in the first half, Jim Taylor fumbled deep in Green Bay territory. Bobby Boyd picked up the loose ball and carried it to the Packer 4-yard line.

Gary Cuozzo, playing quarterback for the Colts in place of the injured John Unitas, threw the ball toward fullback Jerry Hill. Packer fans breathed a sigh of relief when Green Bay linebacker Dave Robinson intercepted the pass. Then they began to cheer as he took off down the field. He went 87 yards before being hauled down from behind. With 14 seconds left in the period, Starr threw to Boyd Dowler for a touchdown, and the Packers were ahead at the half, 21–13.

Green Bay dominated in the third quarter, methodically grinding out yardage in the ball-control style of play that was their trademark. Hornung carried, then Taylor, then Taylor again. Hornung scored his third touchdown of the day on a nine-yard run. Already he had scored more touchdowns than he had all season. As he went into the end zone, a defender pushed Hornung, who slipped right off the field, down the steps and into the baseball dugout at the end of the field.

It looked for a moment as if Hornung had broken his neck. But he was only shaken up. A few plays later he was carrying the ball into the end zone again, this time on a two-yard plunge. With the score Green Bay 35, Baltimore 13, it looked like a rout for the Packers.

Led by blocker Jerry Kramer (64), Hornung (5) looks for an opening in the Colt defense.

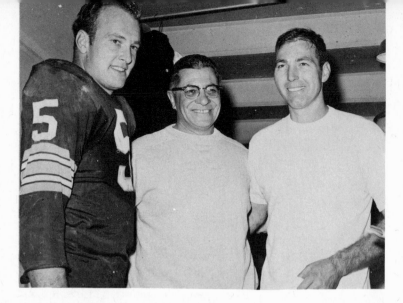

After the game Hornung poses with coach Vince Lombardi and quarterback Bart Starr.

But Baltimore wouldn't give up. Quarterback Cuozzo, who had suffered a shoulder separation during the third quarter, returned in the last period to direct the Colts to a pair of touchdowns. With six minutes left to play, Baltimore trailed by only seven points.

Two plays after taking the Colt kickoff, Green Bay had a third down with nine yards to go on its own 35-yard line. Once again Starr called for a pass to Hornung. The Golden Boy was all alone when he caught the ball on the Baltimore 40 and headed for the goal line—en route to his fifth touchdown of the day.

That was the fifth and last touchdown Hornung scored that day, as the Packers won 42–27. Green Bay went on to the division championship, the league championship and the first Super Bowl. But perhaps more important, Hornung had proved that the tarnished Golden Boy could still be a winner.

19.
Kicker's Day

What's the biggest game in football? Many would say it's the Army-Navy game, the annual meeting between the United States Military Academy at West Point, New York, and the Naval Academy at Annapolis, Maryland. Army and Navy have been playing each other since before 1900, and the list of players includes such military greats as Douglas MacArthur and Dwight Eisenhower and football greats like Glenn Davis and Roger Staubach.

But the heroes of the Army-Navy game don't always become great generals or professional football players. One such hero was Ed Garbisch.

It was November 29, 1924. Football was just becoming a national pastime, and more than 80,000 people trooped to Baltimore's new Municipal Stadium by trolley, by automobile and on foot to see the game. Among the crowd were President and Mrs. Calvin Coolidge. The Commander-in-Chief would sit on the Army side during the first half and with the Navy during the second to show his neutrality. But few others in the crowd were neutral.

The Midshipmen from Navy had come down to the game from nearby Annapolis by the thousands. The Cadets from West Point arrived by train to cheer their classmates on. No matter how the teams did in their other games, the Army-Navy confrontation was the high point of the year. Both teams always gave a little bit extra to take the victory from their arch-rivals.

The Army fans were a little worried that day, however. Their star, running back Lighthorse Harry Wilson, had been injured. He would play, but no one expected him to play his best. Could Army hold on to win anyway?

In the locker room before the game, Cadet Ed Garbisch was putting on his uniform. Ed was the captain of the Army team and its center. Although he was recognized as one of the best players on the team, it hardly seemed that he could win the game single-handed at center. Still, Garbisch was also the Army kicker, so if the team could move him close enough, he might score a point or two after touchdowns or on field goals.

Ed Garbisch had a special reason for wanting to win. His father was very ill, yet had gotten up out of bed to see the game. He had sent a note to Ed with his best wishes. And as Ed put on his pads, he stuck the note—and a lucky four-leaf clover—between his thigh pad and his leg for good luck. Then he ran out on the field and led the Army squad in warm-up calisthenics.

Ed booted the opening kickoff to the Navy 5-yard line, and after the runback the Midshipmen started play on their own 20. The first play was a pass, and Army intercepted. It was the first big break of the game, but the Cadets couldn't seem to take advantage of it. After three plays they had lost a few yards to the bigger Navy line.

Now it was fourth down, and Ed Garbisch went back to attempt a field goal from his 30-yard line. Modern kickers need a holder, but Garbisch didn't. He was a drop-kick specialist. He took the long snap from center and dropped the ball as if to punt. But his kicking foot didn't touch the ball until a split-second after the ball had touched the ground. Ed could get off amazingly strong kicks this way, but this time the big Navy linemen were there to block the attempt. The Cadet fans groaned.

On the next series of downs Army recovered a Navy fumble. But again the Army offense was throttled and again Garbisch went back to try a field goal, this time from the 40. The attempt fell short, and the Army fans grumbled. It seemed unlikely that Garbisch would be a hero today. Midway in the second quarter Garbisch got his third try for a field goal and

105

missed again. Army was still scoreless. The only thing they could boast about was that the smaller Army line had held Navy scoreless, too.

Then late in the quarter Army's Gus Farwick blocked a Navy punt. Ed Garbisch fell on the ball at the Navy 41-yard line, but the Army fans weren't very hopeful—the Cadets had already muffed several chances like this. This time, however, the offense managed to move the ball inside the Navy 20 before being stopped. On fourth down, Garbisch went back once again. The kick was good, and Army took a 3–0 lead.

The Cadets' good fortune was almost forgotten a few minutes later. On a play from scrimmage, Lighthorse Harry Wilson reinjured his leg and was out of the game. Although the half ended with Army still leading, the Cadets had lost their big offensive threat. They anticipated the second half with some concern.

Halfway through the third quarter, Navy still hadn't scored. Then Army's Tiny Hewitt intercepted another Navy pass. The Middies were certainly giving Army enough chances, but once again Army couldn't move the ball. On fourth down Garbisch stepped back to try his fifth field goal of the day from the 42-yard line. It was a booming kick, and it was good! Army 6, Navy 0.

On the first play after the kickoff the hapless Navy quarterback threw another interception. Army drove to the 11-yard line, then ran into a fourth down situation. The 80,000 fans watched the familiar figure of Ed

Garbisch line up nine yards behind the line of scrimmage. Again his kick was good. The thousands of Army rooters cheered Garbisch as he got set to kick off. He had been the only man on either team to score.

Perhaps Ed's biggest achievement of the day was rallying the Army defense again and again to keep Navy away from the goal. To the end of the game, Navy never got close enough to score. In the fourth quarter Garbisch intercepted another Navy pass and later kicked a fourth field goal to make the final score 12–0.

It took Garbisch nearly an hour to get away from the mob of Army fans on the field after the game. They tore off pieces of his jersey, his helmet and even his special kicking shoe as mementos of the occasion. When he finally reached the locker room he dropped to a bench, exhausted. As he started to take off the remnants of his uniform, the note from his father fell to the floor.

Surprisingly, the note was still in one piece, but the four-leaf clover was missing! Had it fallen out during those warm-up calisthenics? Whatever he had done that day—four field goals, a fumble recovery and an interception—must have been the result of his own talent and determination. Lady Luck had deserted him even before the game started.

Army coach John McEwan had the most simple explanation. "Garbisch is the best center West Point ever had," he said.

20.
Crack in the Granite

"California here we come," sang the Fordham University fans at Yankee Stadium. It was Thanksgiving Day, 1936, and the Fordham Rams, undefeated throughout the season, were practically on their way to Pasadena, California, to play in the Rose Bowl on New Year's Day. All they had to do to be sure of a Rose Bowl bid was beat the New York University Violets today.

Fordham was no ordinary football team. The men playing the line for the Rams were known as the "Seven Blocks of Granite." Not only was the team undefeated, but this great line had not even given up a single touchdown all year. The "Block of Granite" who would become most famous was Vince Lombardi, who would one day become the great coach of the Green Bay Packers.

Fordham's famous line, the Seven Blocks of Granite. Vince Lombardi is third from left.

New York University, on the other hand, had had a dismal season. The Violets had opened the year with a 60–0 loss to Ohio State. Then they lost to North Carolina and Carnegie Tech and managed only to tie Georgetown. The big surprise this Thanksgiving Day would be if NYU could put any points on the scoreboard.

Cold weather and snow flurries didn't keep 50,000 fans away from the stadium. Fans from both of the local schools came out to cheer their teams. The NYU backers were hoping against hope that the Violets could at least make a good showing. The confident Fordham fans were there to see the Seven Blocks of Granite on their way to the Rose Bowl.

Midway through the second period, the surprising NYU team started to move with some help from one of

109

football's traditionally unsung players—the punter. Violet kicker Howard Dunney had been averaging 50 yards a punt for the Violets, and against Fordham his punting kept NYU in good field position by continually driving Fordham back toward its own goal.

One of Dunney's second-quarter punts put Fordham back on its own 5-yard line. Then the Rams were forced to punt from their end zone. The kick traveled only to the Fordham 44, and NYU's Bernie Bloom returned the ball nine yards to the 35.

Bloom, in at quarterback for NYU, cut over his right tackle on first down for five yards. He picked up four more yards on the next down. The Violets may have had a miserable season, but they didn't seem afraid of Fordham's granite line.

On third-and-one, Bloom went to the air with a six-yard toss to George Savarese, who caught the ball at the 20 and carried it nine more yards before being tackled. Now the Violets had a first down on the Fordham 11-yard line.

On the very next play, Harry Shorter burst out of the Violet backfield over left tackle on an inside reverse play. The fans watched in amazement as Shorter put a crack in the granite and battled his way to the Fordham goal line. Shorter was stopped short of the goal, but he had picked up a first down on the one-yard line. NYU would have four chances to become the only team to score a touchdown against Fordham in 1936.

110

On the first down play, Bloom tried to go up the middle for the score. Lombardi, Pierce, Paquin and Franco combined for the stop. Bloom came right back with the same play on second down. Once again the Fordham defense held. The ball hadn't advanced a fraction of an inch. It was third down and the one yard was starting to look very long.

On the next play, NYU halfback Milt Miller took the snap from center and headed to the right side of the Fordham line while the rest of the backfield moved to the left. Then he stopped suddenly and threw a lateral to Savarese, who was waiting behind the NYU blockers on the left flank. He slanted inside the Fordham end, twisted away from the tackler and went in for the touchdown. The Violets converted the extra point and led their intra-city rivals 7–0.

The Fordham fans weren't really worried that their great team was in trouble. A few minutes later George McKnight passed to Joe Woltowski for a Fordham touchdown. The Rams failed to make the extra point, making the score 7–6 in favor of NYU. But there was still plenty of time left in the game. Yet all through the second half NYU's defense was as strong as Fordham's and Dunney continued to punt well, keeping the Rams deep in their own territory. When the game ended, the score was still NYU 7, Fordham 6.

The legendary Fordham team had given up its first and only touchdown of the season. It had also lost the game and an invitation to the Rose Bowl.

21.
California Classic

One of the most remarkable games of all time was played on January 2, 1902. It involved one of the great teams in sports history, a colorful coach, a new football tradition and a surprising ending.

The team was from the University of Michigan. Its 1901 season had been not just impressive, but overwhelming. The team had played ten games and won ten, scoring 501 points and allowing not a single point to its opponents. The sportswriters were calling it the "Point-a-Minute" team.

On October 25 the Wolverines scored their biggest win—128–0 against the University of Buffalo. In that game Michigan scored 22 touchdowns and amassed a total of 1,261 yards on the ground (the forward pass had not yet been invented). At one point a Buffalo

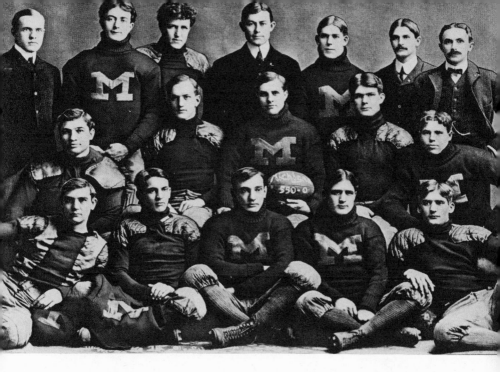

The Michigan Point-A-Minute team. Coach Yost is at top center, and runner Willie Heston is in the middle row at far right.

player came out of the game and staggered over to the Michigan bench.

"Son, you're on the wrong side," the Michigan coach said.

"Oh, no I ain't," the Buffalo player replied, and sat down on the bench.

When the 128–0 score was printed in the Buffalo newspapers, the students wouldn't believe it. They thought the report from Michigan was a hoax. But when the players returned, the fans soon learned the awful truth.

113

The Michigan coach was Fielding H. Yost and some said the "H" stood for "Hurry Up," the coach's favorite expression. He shouted it to his players whether they were scrimmaging at practice, playing in a game or boarding a train.

Yost drove his team constantly, assuring that they would be in better shape than any opponent. Then he added a few trick plays. One of his favorites was called Old 83. The team would line up strong to the right side. Then the quarterback would get the snap from center and fake a hand-off to the fullback, who ran around the right side with the whole blocking for him. Just as the pile-up started, the quarterback would hand the ball to Willie Heston, the team's great running back, and he would race downfield on the left side.

Heston was so fast that in match races against Archie Hahn—who would one day win two Olympic gold medals in the 100-meter dash—Heston would be ahead after 50 yards. He was also a great broken-field runner, and Old 83 was his favorite play.

Football fans around the country knew how great the Michigan team was. What they wanted to know was why the Wolverines were planning to play football the day after New Year's. The season had ended in November, and no one had ever heard of a game in the middle of winter.

The New Year's game was the project of an organization in far-off Pasadena, California. Every year the town sponsored a New Year's festival. Townspeople decorated their carriages with roses and other flowers and had a parade. Now the festival committee wanted to add a football game to the celebration. They invited Michigan, the best team in the country, to play Stanford, the best team in the West in a "Tournament of Roses."

Coach Yost eagerly accepted the invitation. Before coming to Michigan he had been the coach at Stanford, and he welcomed a meeting with his former team. Besides, the game would give the men from Michigan a chance to leave the cold for a few days. When the team boarded the train for the long ride west it was ten degrees below zero. When they arrived in Pasadena, the temperature was 85 degrees.

Hurry Up Yost wasted no time in putting his charges through long, hard practice drills to make sure they still had their stamina. He worried that the heat would wear his boys down.

The day of the game was hot and dry. A crowd of 8,000 fans waited in long lines before entering the stands. Many who had reserved-seat tickets found their places taken by fans who had sneaked in over the fence. Many watched the game standing along the sides of the field.

At three o'clock, after the Tournament of Roses Parade, the game got under way. Stanford had lost only one game all season—by a 2–0 score to arch-rival California—but was still the underdog to the Point-a-Minute team.

For the first 22 minutes of the game, the teams

115

played to a standstill. Then with the ball on the Stanford 29-yard line, Michigan lined up in field-goal formation. But it was one of Yost's trick plays—Old 83. The Michigan players swung out to the right, and the fullback appeared to be running right with the ball. Then, just as the pile-up started, Willie Heston tucked the ball into the crook of his arm and started downfield. He wasn't tackled until he reached the 8-yard line. Four plays later, fullback Neil Snow plowed into the end zone and the Wolverines took the lead (the touchdown was worth five points). Michigan soon scored twice more and led 17–0 at half time.

In the second half Michigan ran poor Stanford off the field. Heston ran around the Stanford defense and Snow ran through it. With ten minutes remaining to play, Snow had scored five touchdowns and Heston had gained 170 yards on 18 carries. The score was Michigan 49, Stanford 0.

The Big Red of Stanford had never threatened the Michigan goal line and had been unable to make more than 15 yards on any single play. Thanks to Michigan's conditioning, the Wolverines weren't even tiring, while the Stanford players were about to drop.

Realizing that defeat was inevitable and that the Michigan runners were even getting hard to see in the gathering dust, the Stanford captain, R. S. Fisher, walked over to Hugh White, the Michigan team leader.

"If you are willing, we are ready to quit," he said.

Weeks, Shorts, Snow, Heston, Herrnstein

TACKLE-BACK-RIGHT PLAY.

Copyright 1902
Earle C. Anthony

FIRST TOURNAMENT OF ROSES GAME, MICHIGAN VS STANFORD. PASADENA, JANUARY 1, 1902.

Michigan (at right) runs a play against Stanford in this early sports photograph.

White agreed, providing a final surprise for this unlikely game. Despite the heat, the same eleven Michigan players played the whole game—and they came close to scoring their point-a-minute.

The little town of Pasadena, which would one day grow to be a sizable city, continued to sponsor football on New Year's, calling the game the Rose Bowl. In later years other bowl games were played in other cities. But the very first bowl game set the pattern—and Fielding Yost's amazing Michigan team set the standard for excellence.

22.
Delay of Game

The Illinois players filed quietly into the locker room. They had just stopped an Ohio State scoring threat on the last play of the game and were content to settle for a 26–26 tie, even though it lessened their chances for the Big Ten championship.

Over in the home locker room, the Ohio State players weren't exactly cheering, either. A tie was better than a loss, and the game had been a "moral victory" for the Buckeyes, since they had been the underdogs. But a moral victory wouldn't show up in the standings.

It was November 13, 1943, and as the 36,331 spectators filed out of the stadium in Columbus, Ohio, they rehashed the game, trying to figure out how the Buckeyes could have won.

Illinois had started quickly in the game, scoring early in the first quarter, covering 68 yards on two plays. Minutes later, they had scored again on a 32-yard run and a two-yard plunge over the goal. Ohio State had come right back, scoring on a 51-yard drive, to make the score 12–7. Both teams had scored once in the second period, and the Illini were ahead 19–13 at the half.

The Buckeyes had given the crowd something to cheer about in the third quarter. In a persistent drive of 88 yards on 17 plays, they took the lead for the first time, 20–19. John Stungis, a 17-year-old freshman quarterback made two extra-point kicks for Ohio State, giving them the advantage.

The Buckeyes had kept rolling in the fourth quarter. In another long march, they went 80 yards in 17 plays for the touchdown. Stungis missed the extra point, but the Buckeyes now led, 26–19.

The stronger Illinois team hadn't given up, however. Late in the game, halfback Eddie Bray had rambled 57 yards through the desperate Ohio State defenders, all the way to the one-yard line. Illinois scored from there, and quarterback Don Greenwood kicked the extra point to tie the score, 26–26, with minutes remaining.

The Buckeyes had taken the kickoff and started down the field again, calling plays as quickly as possible. But they lost the ball on downs at the Illinois 20-yard line. The Illini got to the OSU 41-yard line but then lost the ball. The crowd had been frantic as the Buckeyes took over and began a wild drive for the Illinois end zone. But Illinois recovered an Ohio State fumble on the 15-yard line to end the threat with eleven seconds left to play. It seemed that the game was over, but then Illinois fumbled on its first play, and Ohio recovered on the 21-yard line. There were two seconds left—time for one play. The quarterback threw a pass into the end zone as time ran out—incomplete. The scoreboard read: Illinois 26, Ohio State 26.

As the last few fans milled around the nearly empty stadium, a few players—still in uniform—came trotting back onto the field. Then more players from both teams came out. The fans were puzzled. The players lined up on the 21-yard line, where Ohio State had had possession when the game ended. Then the officials moved the ball up to the 16-yard line and the referee signaled offside, pointing toward the Illinois team.

The Illini had eleven men on the field, obviously ready to play defense. Ohio State's place-kicker, young Stungis, was lining up as though to kick a field goal. The referee marked the ball ready for play. The ball was snapped, placed down and kicked—twelve minutes after the game had apparently ended, Ohio State's John Stungis kicked the ball through the uprights. The fans didn't know it yet, but Ohio State had won the game. What was going on?

The officials had ruled that Illinois had been offside on the last play of the game. The players hadn't seen the head linesman signal the infraction and had trooped off the field. But the rules say that a game can't end on a penalty, so the officials had to call the players back from the locker room for one more play.

And though there were few spectators around to see it, underdog Ohio State finally beat Illinois, 29–26.

23.
Comedy of Errors

More than 300 years ago William Shakespeare wrote a play called "A Comedy of Errors."

Shakespeare didn't know anything about football, but the name of the play certainly described the game between the Minnesota Vikings and the San Francisco 49ers on October 25, 1964. Of course, many of the 31,845 fans in San Francisco's Kezar Stadium that day didn't find the game very funny, but no one could deny that it was a game of errors.

The cast of characters gave a hint of what was to come. The Vikings were a young and inexperienced team, formed in an expansion draft just three years earlier. And although the 49ers had been in the league for a long time, they had somehow managed to remain one of only two teams that had *never* won a National Football League championship.

Their ill-fated confrontation began when Minnesota's Bill Brown fumbled the opening kickoff. San Francisco's Kermit Alexander recovered, and a few plays later, 49er quarterback John Brodie carried the ball into the end zone. The first error had put the home team ahead, 7–0.

The 49ers kicked off again, and again the poor Vikings lost the ball on a fumble. They fumbled a third time when they got the ball again, tying a league record for most consecutive fumbles at the start of a game. But the 49ers couldn't turn these fumbles into scores— they were making errors of their own. After the third fumble, 49er quarterback John Brodie threw a pass right into the arms of Viking linebacker Roy Winston. This time Minnesota managed to hold on to the ball and moved it close enough for Fred Cox to make a 41-yard field goal. At the end of the first quarter the 49ers led 7–3.

Early in the second period both teams gave up their pratfalls for a few minutes and scored touchdowns to make the score 14–10, San Francisco. But the rest of the period had the San Francisco fans groaning. Twice the 49ers drove toward the goal line, and twice quarterback Brodie threw passes to Viking defenders in the end zone. These interceptions cost the 49ers 14 points. On the last play of the first half, however, San Francisco's Tommy Davis kicked a 37-yard field goal, and the 49ers led at half time, 17–10.

After intermission both teams continued their bumbling ways. San Francisco took the kickoff, then Brodie threw an interception. Moments later, Minnesota's Fran Tarkenton threw an interception himself. The Vikings scored on a long field goal in the third period, but it seemed that both teams were trying hard to lose.

The crowd was unhappy—the 49er lead had shrunk to four points and Brodie had thrown four interceptions. The fans wanted a new quarterback. "We want Mira!" they chanted. San Francisco coach Jack Christiansen may have been unhappy with Brodie, too. Early in the fourth quarter, Brodie came out and was replaced by back-up quarterback George Mira.

Minnesota's Fran Tarkenton gets a big rush from the 49ers.

If the fans expected much improvement from Mira, they were quickly disappointed. On his second offensive play, Mira was forced to hurry a pass. The ball was picked off by Viking Roy Winston—his third interception of the day. He returned it to the San Francisco 11-yard line. Three plays later Tarkenton carried the ball into the end zone, and the Vikings took the lead, 20–17.

Minutes later, Mira was hit hard by Viking defensive end Jim Marshall, and the ball popped loose. Carl Eller, the other Minnesota defensive end, scooped it up and rambled 45 yards for a touchdown, putting Minnesota ahead 27–17.

Following the kickoff, it looked as if Mira finally had the 49er offense on the move. Then he threw a pass to running back Billy Kilmer (who later became a leading quarterback himself). Kilmer caught the ball but was hit so hard that he fumbled. That was fumble number two for the 49ers, who had already watched five of their passes go astray. The Vikings, with three fumbles, seemed to be in slightly better shape. But the game wasn't over yet. The best—or worst—was still to come.

When Kilmer lost the ball, the Vikings' Jim Marshall swooped in, picked it up and headed for the goal line. He was out in the clear, and the crowd went wild as he chugged toward the end zone. After crossing the goal, he triumphantly flung the ball into the air.

Then, as Marshall saw his teammates running to-

ward him, he had a terrible thought: the Vikings were playing away from home, in San Francisco. The crowd should not be cheering his touchdown.

And they weren't. The jubilant hometown fans were cheering the two points going up on the 49er side of the scoreboard. Marshall had just run 60 yards—the wrong way. Instead of a Minnesota touchdown, it was a safety for San Francisco, making the score 27–19. Marshall's error was the biggest—and funniest—of the day.

But Marshall had the last laugh. The Vikings gave up just one more field goal and won the game, 27–22. The hometown fans went away grumbling, and few of the players cared to remember their afternoon of mistakes. But looking back, five interceptions, five lost fumbles *and* a wrong-way run certainly made the game a comedy of errors.

The Vikings' Jim Marshall runs into the end zone untouched (top). The referee signals a safety for the 49ers at center as Marshall realizes his mistake. At bottom, Marshall hangs his head in embarrassment—he had run the wrong way.

24.
Young Number 6

The 51,000 fans in West Lafayette, Indiana, were getting a little nervous. They had come to watch the Purdue Boilermakers pick up an easy win over an underdog team from Bowling Green State University. It was September 16, 1972, the first game of the new season. But things weren't going quite as planned. Although Purdue was one of the top 20 teams in the country and a leading contender for the Big Ten championship, the Falcons from little Bowling Green didn't seem at all impressed.

Things had started off badly for the mighty Boilermakers when a Purdue fumble was recovered by the Falcons. Bowling Green scored on the very next play with a 20-yard pass from Reid Lamport to Roger Wallace.

128

Young Bowling Green
place-kicker Don Taylor.

Then, over the loudspeakers came the announce-
ment: Number 6, Don Taylor, would attempt the
extra point. But there was no Number 6 listed on the
Bowling Green roster. Even Falcon fans were still
trying to identify him when his kick sailed over the
goal posts and the Falcons were ahead 7–0.

The Boilermakers stormed right back, and just
about a minute later, Skip Peterson exploded on a 40-
yard touchdown run to tie the score at 7-all.

Then with five seconds remaining in the first quarter, another Purdue fumble deep in its own territory
gave the Falcons another chance. Bowling Green's Bill
Pittman snatched up the ball on the 7-yard line and
carried it into the end zone. Once more Taylor—or
"What's-his-name?" as the fans were calling him—
made the extra point to give the Falcons a 14–7 lead.

For Purdue, this game was to be a warm-up for a

129

tough schedule in the Big Ten. But the Boilermakers couldn't seem to even the score. Finally, with 1:28 left in the half, Purdue halfback Otis Armstrong sprinted 16 yards for a touchdown. The extra point tied the game, and shortly afterward the half ended.

In the third quarter Purdue kept the upper hand on the field, but the surprising Bowling Green defense wouldn't allow a score. The Falcons couldn't score either, however, and Don Taylor hadn't made any more appearances.

Then late in the period came the crucial play, adding another weird note to the proceedings. Bowling Green had the ball on its own 17-yard line. It was fourth down, 17 yards to go. Punter Eddie McCoy went back almost to his own goal line, ready for the punt.

McCoy took the snap from center and rushed his kick to avoid a blocked punt. The ball went straight up in the air, and came down a few feet from McCoy. It bounced right into his arms just as the Purdue lineman rushed toward him. McCoy ran for his life. Before anyone could catch him, he had reached the 38-yard line and gotten a first down. The kick had not gone beyond the line of scrimmage, so McCoy's run (Bowling Green's longest of the day) was perfectly legal.

The Falcons took advantage of their lucky break. They marched downfield—with the help of some big penalties against Purdue—all the way to the Purdue 11-yard line. Then the Boilermakers' defense finally held. It was fourth down.

The stands began buzzing again as Number 6 trotted out to attempt a field goal. Once again the public address announcer informed the crowd that Don Taylor would try the kick. Who was this player who had a chance to upset Purdue?

The fans would have been surprised if they had known his story. Taylor was about to become a freshman at Bowling Green. He had never even attended a lecture at the school, since classes wouldn't start for nearly two weeks. His football background was strange, too. Taylor had been with the team just three days, and he was lucky to be on the squad at all. As a high school senior in Canton, Ohio, he had been a punter and place-kicker on a team that had won three games, lost six and tied one. Taylor had averaged 38.5 yards a punt and made nine of twelve point-after-touchdown attempts. But he hadn't kicked a field goal all year. As he said, "We never got close enough for me to try."

Now his new team was close enough, and now Taylor had a chance to put the Falcons ahead. His field goal attempt, 29 yards from the crossbar, was good. The Falcons took the lead, 17–14.

The Bowling Green defense held fast the rest of the way, and the result was an upset victory over the 18th-ranked Boilermakers. The winning drive had been started by a punter who ran back his own kick. And the winning field goal had been made by an unlisted player who was not yet a student and who had never before kicked a field goal.

131

25.

Big Game in San Francisco

They came on horseback and trolley, on foot, by buggy and bicycle. More than 20,000 fans were heading through the hilly streets of San Francisco to the Haight Street Grounds, a converted baseball diamond, for the first intercollegiate football game on the West Coast.

It was March 19, 1892—an unlikely time of the year for football—when the University of California met the football club of the new Leland Stanford University. The University of California had been playing football for ten years, mostly against high school and club teams. The Blue and Gold Bears issued a challenge to the Stanford students early in the school year, but Stanford's team captain, John R. Whittemore (who was also student body president), didn't think his squad would be ready to play a Thanksgiving Day game. So the big game was scheduled for March.

Stanford had practiced for the game by playing three scrimmage games against local high schools. The Stanford team manager, a young man named Hoover, had collected enough money at those practice games to buy athletic equipment and the Cardinal-red jerseys that are still a Stanford trademark.

Part of Hoover's duties included handling the sale of tickets for the big game. The seating capacity of the Haight Street Grounds was 15,000. But Hoover had not expected a full house and ordered only 10,000 tickets printed.

When 20,000 fans showed up, Hoover scurried about trying to make up for the lack of tickets. He charged people as they entered the field and made sure no one got in without paying. One of the problems was the money. Paper money was scarce, and coins were the common currency. The coins were spilling all over the place, so Hoover had to round up wash tubs and dish pans to haul away the proceeds.

Meanwhile, on the field, the teams were loosening up before the opening kickoff when suddenly they realized there was no football. A sporting goods dealer in the crowd offered to furnish one. He hopped on his horse and headed back to his store. An hour later he was back with a ball. It wasn't really a football and certainly not a regulation football, but it was the best

133

he could do. It looked like an elongated soccer ball, with an extra-bouncy bladder inside of it.

At four o'clock, with the sun slowly sinking in the West, captain Whittemore of Stanford and captain George Foulks of California walked to midfield for the coin toss. The winner of the toss usually chose to kick off. Under the rules of the day, the ball only had to be touched by the kicker before it could be recovered by either team, so the kicking team almost always recovered it.

Stanford won the toss and Whittemore chose—much to everyone's surprise—to defend the West goal. He figured that the setting sun might provide some problems for the California team. Whittemore also thought that the odd ball they were using would be hard to control. So even if California kicked off, they would have a tough time handling it. California recovered the opening kickoff, but just as Whittemore had thought, the Bears fumbled a few plays later and Stanford recovered.

Using a variation of the flying wedge—where blockers formed a tight V by holding on to each others' jerseys—Stanford struck quickly with Carl Clemans carrying 45 yards for the first touchdown, which was then worth four points. Stanford, with Whittemore, Clemans and Paul Downing taking turns carrying the ball on double reverses and the flying wedge, ran the California defense ragged. They added two more touchdowns and one kick-after-touchdown (worth two points) to take a 14–0 lead by the time the first 45-minute half ended.

There was a ten-minute rest period and then another solid 45 minutes of football. The experienced California players fought back in the second half, but were able to score only ten points.

The final score of the game was Stanford 14, California 10. Neither team had made a substitution in the hour and a half of playing time.

Team manager Hoover had been so busy protecting the gate receipts, he didn't even get a chance to see the game, but he was amazed and pleased when he heard the final score. Hoover went on to become an engineer, a government official and finally President of the United States, but he always remembered with special pleasure his hectic day as manager of the Stanford team.

26.

Vikings' First Game

In the 1960s pro football exploded into prominence. During that decade the number of teams doubled and people all over the country became pro football fans. One result of the rapid expansion was that aging veterans were able to play for an extra season or two. In addition, there were many more chances for rookies to make the professional rosters. When a new team was admitted to the league, it received the least-wanted players from established clubs—mostly has-beens and never-weres. It was no wonder that these expansion teams finished at the bottom of the league in their first few seasons.

One of the first expansion teams in the NFL was the Minnesota Vikings. As they prepared for their first National Football League game on September 11,

1961, they too had a rag-tag team that even Minnesota fans couldn't take seriously. Their opponents, on the other hand, were the Chicago Bears—charter members of the league and contenders for NFL championships for 40 years. The Chicago coach was George Halas, who was also the founder and chief owner of the team and had decades of experience as a coach.

Minnesota was even guided by a rookie coach, Norm Van Brocklin. The Dutchman, as fans called him, had been an outstanding quarterback with the Los Angeles Rams and the Philadelphia Eagles. But coaching was new to him.

The Bears' line-up was studded with stars, players who had made the all-league teams. The Vikings had a few great names in their line-up, too, but these were stars who were past their prime. Many of the other Vikings were untested first- and second-year men.

The game hardly seemed like a fair match, but to the surprise and delight of the 32,000 fans in Minnesota's Municipal Stadium, Minnesota took a 3–0 lead early in the first quarter on a twelve-yard field goal by rookie Mike Mercer.

The Vikings kept up their surprises, driving into Bear territory the next time they had the ball. This time they stalled on the 19-yard line and a field goal attempt was wide of the uprights. Still, the Vikings were doing well.

When Chicago took over, a pass from quarterback Billy Wade was partially deflected and intercepted by

Viking defensive halfback Clancy Osborne, who carried the ball to the Chicago 20-yard line.

Coach Van Brocklin, worried because his team had failed to get into the end zone with two golden opportunities, put in his second-string quarterback, a rookie named Francis Tarkenton.

Van Brocklin had worked hard with Tarkenton, teaching him how to "read" pro defenses; how to anticipate defensive shifts; how to attack with a series of moves rather than with a single play; how to best use his own players against weaknesses in the defense.

All of this may have bewildered young Tarkenton. In the first series of downs he couldn't move the Viking offense in to score. Tarkenton seemed to learn from his experience, however. Two minutes into the second quarter he flipped a 14-yard scoring pass to Bob Schnelker, and the Vikings were ahead 10-0. Chicago retaliated quickly, driving 66 yards in 13 plays for a touchdown. The Bears had the momentum as the first half ended, but the Vikings were ahead 10-6—an amazing performance for their first league game.

The Bears received the kickoff to start the second half, and on the first play from scrimmage, Willie Galimore carried over left tackle. The Vikings' rookie linebacker Rip Hawkins crashed into Galimore with such force that the ball popped loose. Rich Mostardi recov-

Rookie quarterback Fran Tarkenton consults with Viking coach Norm Van Brocklin.

ered for the Vikings on the Chicago 27-yard line.
Three plays later, Tarkenton lofted a pass to Jerry
Reichow deep in the end zone, and the Vikings in-
creased their lead to 17–6.

A few minutes later it began to look like a rout.
Tarkenton and Reichow combined on a 47-yard pass
play that put the ball two yards from the Chicago goal
line. The Vikings fumbled on two of their next three
plays but managed to recover the ball each time. On
fourth down, Tarkenton rolled out and rifled a pass to
Hugh McElhenny, who was waiting in the end zone.
The score was now 24–6.

Tarkenton scored a touchdown on a two-yard
sneak following another Viking interception, and then
Fran threw his fourth touchdown pass of the afternoon
to Dave Middleton to make the score 37–6. The Bears
added a touchdown late in the game to make the final
score Minnesota 37, Chicago 13.

The upstarts had beaten the veterans. Fran Tarkenton, a rookie quarterback, and Norm Van Brocklin, a rookie head coach, had led a rookie team to victory in its very first league game. The Vikings won
only two more games all year, while the Bears were
challenging for the division lead. But the satisfaction of
that first big win stayed with the Vikings all year long.

27.
Way Down Upon
the Sewanee

Twenty-five men—almost one quarter of the entire student body—greeted new coach Herman Suter early in September of 1899 at the University of the South. Suter, once a football star and all-around athlete at Princeton, had come to the small school in Sewanee, Tennessee, to build a football team that would challenge the best teams in the South. Among the 25 candidates who turned out were seven letter winners. In the final game of the 1898 season Sewanee had upset Vanderbilt, generally considered the best team in the South. So Suter started work with an eager group of players.

There was one problem, however. Vanderbilt wasn't on the 1899 schedule because of a dispute about the gate receipts. How could the team from Sewanee

The 1899 Sewanee football team. Manager Lea and coach Suter are at top center.

claim to be the best in the South without playing the old champions from Vanderbilt? Team manager Luke Lea was assigned to make up a schedule that would prove to everyone that Sewanee (as the University was called) was *the* best in the region.

And some schedule it was! Sewanee opened the season against Georgia on Saturday, October 1. They won 12–0. They took Sunday off, but on Monday they played Georgia Tech, rolling up a 32–0 victory.

During the next four weeks, Sewanee played only two games, handing Tennessee a 46–0 whipping and traveling to Memphis to defeat Southern Presbyterian (now Southwestern University) 54–0.

The Tigers then embarked on a road trip unique in the history of college play. On November 7, 1899, twelve members of the Sewanee team gathered at the tiny train depot in Sewanee. All that manager Lea

142

would say was that they were headed for Texas. Lea even loaded a barrel of spring water onto the train for the team.

Two days later, on November 9, the Sewanee Tigers met the University of Texas at Austin and won 12–0. After the game Lea got the team back on the train. They were going to Houston to play Texas A&M the following day. Sewanee won that one 32–0. Lea's next surprise was another overnight trip, to New Orleans, where Tulane was the opponent. Sewanee won its third game in three days by the score of 23–0. The fourth day was Sunday, and no game was scheduled, but Monday they were off to Baton Rouge to play Louisiana State. Sewanee won that, too, 34–0.

Lea then told his tired players that they were heading back to Tennessee. But there was a catch. Along the way they would stop at Jackson, Mississippi, to play against the University of Mississippi. The strain of traveling 3,000 miles in less than a week and playing five football games in six days was beginning to show. Sewanee scored only twelve points. But the Mississippi team—like every other opponent Sewanee had faced— was held scoreless.

Coach Suter gave the players a well-deserved rest when they returned to the campus. Suter and team captain Diddy Seibels also had a long talk with Lea, criticizing his ridiculous scheduling. Lea's only answer was that Sewanee had won all the games and shut out every opponent.

After the layoff, the Tigers tuned up with a 71–0 rout of Cumberland. Then, on Thanksgiving Day, they traveled to Montgomery, Alabama, to play unbeaten Auburn in what was called "The Battle of the South." Each team drew large groups of supporters. The cheerleaders—a new development in college football—even had to use megaphones to make themselves heard.

Coach Johnny Heisman's Auburn team was noted for its great speed. When the game started, it looked as though the Plainsmen were going to run Sewanee right off the field. Only the extraordinary punting of Sewanee's Simkins kept the game from getting out of hand.

Auburn scored first to take a 5–0 lead. Shortly afterward, a poor Auburn punt gave Sewanee the ball on the Auburn 20-yard line. Three plays later the Tigers evened the score at 5–5. Auburn retaliated the next time it had the ball, as quarterback Ed Huguley did most of the ball-carrying. He scored the go-ahead touchdown which made it Auburn 10, Sewanee 5.

Late in the game, with time running out and darkness beginning to fall, Simkins punted to the Auburn 5-yard line. Then Auburn fumbled and Sewanee recovered. Now Sewanee had one chance to live up to their claim of being the best in the South. Otherwise all their travels would be in vain. But they couldn't score, and Auburn took over on downs.

On Auburn's first play, Huguley fumbled again.

Sewanee recovered on the one-yard line. They had miraculously been given one more chance to win. Simkins took the ball into the end zone. He then kicked the winning extra point. Sewanee was the champion of the South, defeating Auburn 11–10. Although Sewanee had finally been scored upon after eleven games, they were still undefeated.

Master schedule-maker Luke Lea was still up to his old tricks, however. The Monday after the Auburn game, Sewanee traveled to North Carolina to play the University of North Carolina. Simkins provided the only scoring of the day, kicking a field goal worth five points. The exhausted Sewanee team won 5–0, and were recognized as the best in the South.

28.
Free Kick

It gets cold in northern Wisconsin in November—very cold. But that never stops a Green Bay Packer fan. Lambeau Field in Green Bay, Wisconsin, was jammed with its usual sellout crowd of 50,861 on November 3, 1968, when the Packers opposed the Chicago Bears. The fans were there to see a crucial game in the NFL Central Division. A victory would put either team into first place.

There were other things that made the game more than the usual Sunday spectacle in Green Bay. For one thing, the Chicago-Green Bay rivalry had always been one of the fiercest in football. Players from both teams understood that if they did nothing else all season, they must win this game.

Another point of special interest was that both teams had new coaches. Phil Bengtson was in his first

146

season as Packer coach, trying to live up to the performance of former coach Vince Lombardi, who had won four NFL championships for Green Bay. This was an important game for Bengtson. The Bears' founder-owner George "Papa Bear" Halas had retired as coach, and new Bear coach Jim Dooley was on the spot, too.

Going into the fourth quarter the Bears were three points ahead, 10–7, but Green Bay was poised for a field-goal attempt. On the first play of the period Green Bay kicker Chuck Mercein split the uprights to knot the score at 10–10. The stadium went wild, and the Packer fans wanted more.

The teams exchanged the football through most of the quarter without scoring. With less than two minutes left in the game, the Packers took possession on their own 15-yard line. Green Bay quarterback Bart Starr specialized in last-minute game-saving drives. But today he was having trouble. He threw three incomplete passes in a row. The Packers would have to punt and hope for a tie.

There was just over half a minute left on the scoreboard clock when Green Bay's Donny Anderson got set to punt. Anderson had been kicking well, but this time the ball went only 28 yards from the line of scrimmage. The Bears' Cecil Turner called for a fair catch on the Green Bay 43. With good field position already assured, calling a fair catch reduces the risk of a fumble. Turner managed to hold on to the ball at the Packer 43-yard line.

147

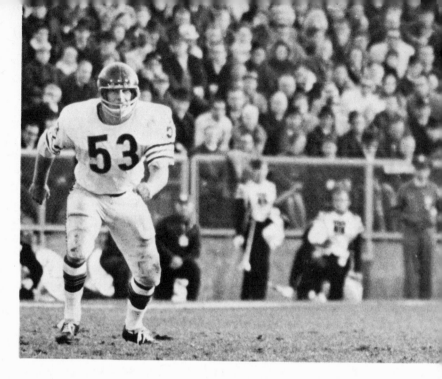

What followed was confusion. Mac Percival, the Bears' place-kicker trotted onto the field. It seemed odd that with time for several plays the Bears would try a field goal from the 43-yard line. Then the referees began consulting with both teams. The Packers began walking toward their own goal. At first the fans thought a penalty had been called. But then they noticed that the Chicago players weren't following the Packers down the field. Then Chicago's Richie Petitbon knelt down at the 43 and set the ball up as if he were holding it for a field-goal kicker. What was going on?

Coach Dooley of the Bears had invoked one of the most unusual and least used rules in football. The rule book says that after a fair catch the team with the ball may put the ball into play either with a standard play

Chicago's Mac Percival takes a rare free kick.

from scrimmage or with a *free kick*. The opposing team must be ten yards away from the ball (that's why the Packers were walking), and if the ball clears the goal posts on the kick, it counts as a field goal.

The Packers and the Green Bay fans watched help-lessly as Chicago kicker Mac Percival got set to kick. No one could rush him or block the kick, so he took his time. His kick was perfect—and Chicago went ahead 13–10.

The Bears kicked off and Packer quarterback Bart Starr had time for two plays. But it was too late to score. Chicago had won the game on a free-kick field goal. Many disappointed Packer fans didn't even know why until they went home and read their rule books.

Index

Page numbers in italics refer to photographs.

INDEX

INDEX

INDEX

153